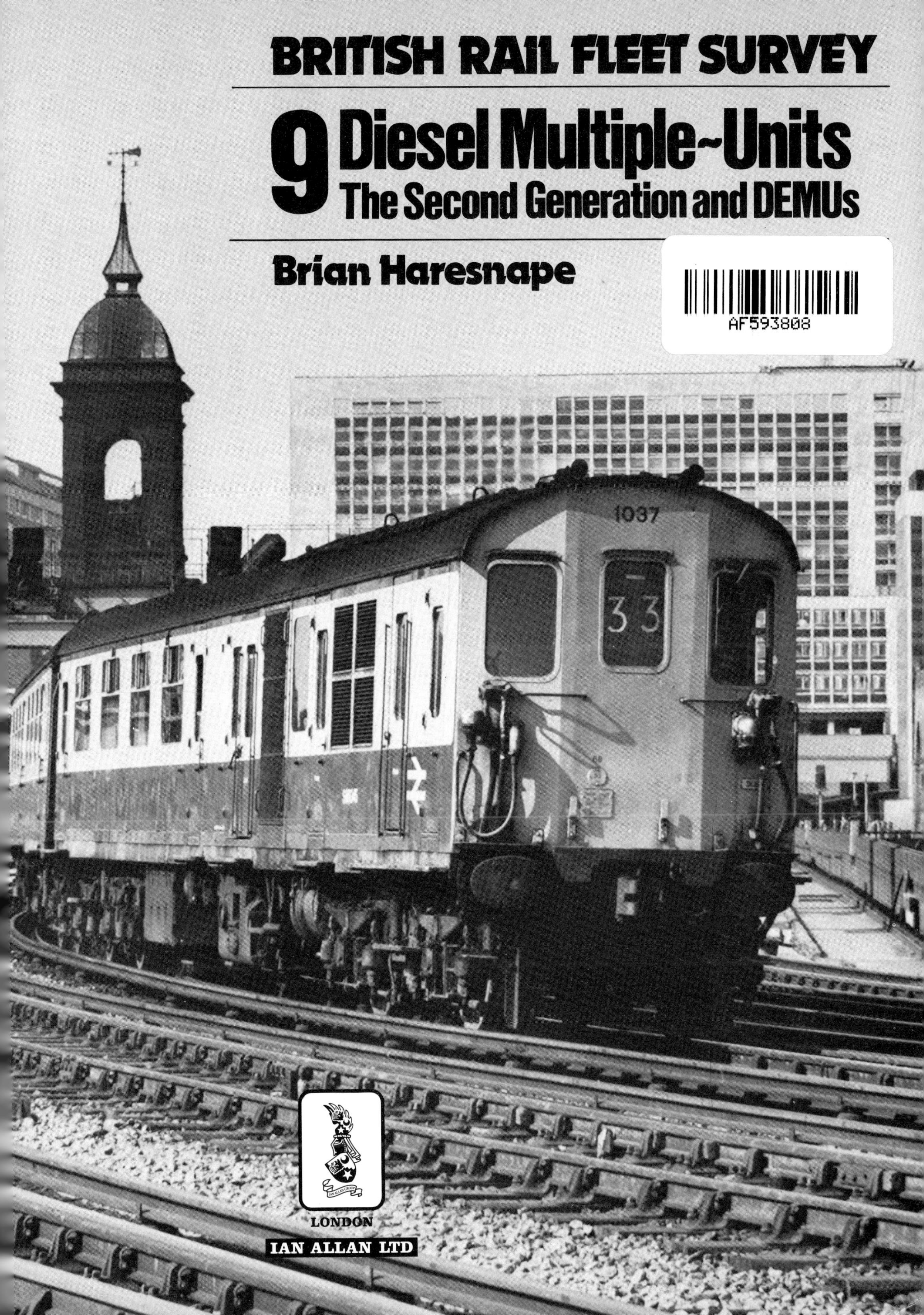
BRITISH RAIL FLEET SURVEY
9 Diesel Multiple~Units
The Second Generation and DEMUs
Brian Haresnape
AF593808
1037
33
LONDON
IAN ALLAN LTD

Contents

First published 1986

ISBN 0 7110 1604 6

Published by Ian Allan Ltd, Shepperton, Surrey; and printed by Ian Allan Printing Ltd at their works at Coombelands in Runnymede, England

Cover:
Class 150/1 'Sprinter' No 150106.
Hugh Ballantyne

Previous page:
Class 203 'Hastings' DEMU No 1037 leaving Charing Cross with the 17.00 to Hastings on 7 June 1976. *Brian Morrison*

Below:
Class 142 units Nos 142039 and 142040 approach Prestatyn on a crew-training duty on 20 February 1986. *Larry Goddard*

Introduction: The Genesis of the British DEMU

IN Part 8 of this series I traced the development of the diesel-mechanical railcar from its 1930s embryonic form until the establishment and subsequent operation of the huge fleet of DMUs which were required by the BR Modernisation Plan. This, I have chosen to call the 'First Generation' because we are now witnessing the swansong of these vehicles, and their DMU fleet replacements are now entering service. However, it was not only the diesel-mechanical railcar that featured in the Modernisation Plan; although it was certainly the more important in sheer numerical order. One Region chose not to utilise the DMU, but to go its own way instead and to develop the diesel-electric power unit for multiple-unit use. This Region was of course, the Southern, and it is this fleet of DEMUs that are first of all to be described in this book. The second part of the book describes the new fleet of DMUs now being introduced — the 'New Generation' — and between the two parts there is an analysis of the various experiments and alternative prototypes that BR and outside industry developed, before deciding upon the 'New Generation' designs.

Let us first of all briefly examine the prewar scene with regard to diesel-electric railcars; having already examined the prewar development of the diesel-mechanicals in Part 8.

It was the London Midland & Scottish Railway that first showed a cautious willingness to experiment with a diesel-electric passenger train, when in 1928 it produced a four-car unit powered by a Beardmore 500hp engine. This was the first such train to appear in Europe. The Beardmore engine (actually being developed for use in the R101 airship) powered two electric traction motors of Dick Kerr/English Electric Co design. The motor bogie was secondhand, from a redundant ex-LNWR London area electric power car. Used in Lancashire, over the Preston-Blackpool line, this quite imposing-looking four-car unit failed to make much of a favourable impression, and was quietly withdrawn when Beardmore ceased to exist, (following the ghastly R101 airship disaster) in 1931. As well as this pioneer LMSR train, Beardmore also contributed to the export market; notably to Spain and Canada, and helped to establish the feasibility of the diesel-electric railcar train; whilst various alternatives using hydraulic or mechanical transmissions were also being produced in Germany, North America and elsewhere.

In 1931 there appeared the first of a trio of single unit diesel-electric railcars designed by Armstrong Whitworth/Sulzer. These were intended to be demonstration vehicles, to be tried out by the 'Big Four' railway companies; of which three — the LMSR, LNER and SR — showed enough interest to warrant the cost of building three prototypes. It is not recorded, to my knowledge, why the GWR showed no interest, but one presumes that some hint of the forthcoming AEC/Hardy Motors diesel-mechanical railcar design had already interested Swindon engineers (see Part 8 of this series) who therefore saw little point in pursuing a diesel-electric alternative, at least for the time being. Of the three cars built, the SR example

Above right:
In 1928 the London Midland & Scottish Railway (LMSR) introduced a diesel-electric four-car train as an experiment, at the suggestion of Beardmore, who manufactured the 500hp engine installed. This diesel engine was similar to those designed for the ill-fated R101 airship. The electrical components were made by English Electric at the former Siemens Co works at Stafford and the motor bogie was from an original LNWR Siemens power car of the London area; placed at the rear end of the power car.

The carriages were former Lancashire & Yorkshire Railway (LYR) electric stock; with one power car altered to carry the power unit. This pioneer DEMU was not very successful, and soon disappeared from the scene, but it created interest in the DEMU concept within English Electric. *British Rail*

Right:
The LMSR *Northumbrian*, was converted as the *Armstrong Shell Express* to operate between London and Castle Bromwich for the duration of the British Industries Fair in 1933. It is seen leaving Euston on a trial working on Tuesday 14 February 1933. *Ian Allan Library*

Left:
Two of the three Armstrong Whitworth/Sulzer DEMUs are seen here in the northeast of England on one of the rare occasions when they ran in multiple. The leading railcar is *Lady Hamilton* which was intended for prototype trials on the Southern Railway, but only paid a brief visit; spending the rest of its days on the London & North Eastern Railway (LNER). The livery was an attractive blue and cream, with gold lining. *LPC*

Below:
The prototype diesel-electric railcar introduced by the English Electric Co in 1933; which ran trials on the LMSR. The power unit was at the other end of the vehicle, above floor level. A trailer carriage is attached in this view to give added accommodation. Note the manually-operated sliding doors to the passenger saloon. *GEC Traction*

Bottom:
English Electric designed and built this 400hp diesel-electric train for the Egyptian State Railways, soon after the end of World War 2. In appearance it strangely foreshadowed the frontal styling of the prototype BR High Speed Train. The new design of four-cylinder diesel engine was known as the 4SRKT and was to become the basis for the Southern Region DEMU fleet designs, in due course.
GEC Traction

(named *Lady Hamilton*, apparently as a tribute to the classic SR 4-6-0 steam locomotive No 850 *Lord Nelson*, introduced in 1926) barely touched SR metals, and spent nearly all its life operating within LNER territory. The LMSR example was at first named *Northumbrian*; of which more anon. The first one to run demonstrations, in 1931, was the LNER example named appropriately *Tyneside Venturer*, (the Armstrong Whitworth works were located on Tyneside) and this impressed the LNER so much that they purchased it in 1932 for regular passenger services in the Scarborough area. The LNER later also purchased *Lady Hamilton* and *Northumbrian*, and ran all three until 1939, when they were stored out of use during the war period, until scrapping in 1944. Storage was probably mainly because of fuel shortages; although these railcars seem to have been giving less satisfactory mechanical performance by this stage of their careers.

In 1933 the LMSR had taken the *Northumbrian* on to their rails as planned, but decided to modify it at their own Wolverton Carriage Works, making it into a luxury buffet bar saloon railcar for only 12 passengers (as compared to the 60 seats provided originally!). The LMSR renamed it the *Armstrong Shell Express*, and in this guise it ran a daily service from London (Euston) to Castle Bromwich, near Birmingham, for select VIP visitors to the British Industries Fair — thereby promoting both the Shell Oil Company *and* Armstrong Whitworth! After this enterprise it was restored to its previous seating arrangement and purchased by the LNER; who alone of the three originally interested parties persevered with the initial trials and tribulations of these three railcars; at one stage, as already stated, obtaining quite satisfactory service. They then became known as the 'Tyneside Venturer' type, and carried LNER numbers as follows:

Left:
The English Electric four-cylinder 4SRKT engine, by then rated at 500hp, is seen here being lowered into the body of one of the power cars of the first six-car DEMU set built at Eastleigh for the SR Hastings line, in January 1957. Two power cars per six-car train gave 1,000hp. No through passenger access was provided between each six-car set, and therefore the engine room was spacious enough to take such a large power unit above floor level; giving it maximum protection. *British Railways*

Below:
'Hastings' unit No 1034 (one of the long-underframe sets, with buffet car) enters Tonbridge station on 22 April 1961 on a Charing Cross-Hastings working. The very plain appearance of these new DEMUs gave rise to considerable criticism when they were first introduced. The set is in the original green livery. *Alec Swain*

No 25 *Tyneside Venturer*, No 224 *Lady Hamilton* and No 232 *Northumbrian*; each wearing a very attractive deep blue and cream livery. They were capable of towing a bogie passenger carriage as a trailer, and (in principle, but rarely in practice) of working in multiple as pairs. With steel bodies upon steel underframes, built by Cravens of Sheffield, these diesel-electrics were not lightweight in concept, but the 250hp six-cylinder Sulzer engine seems to have provided a good power output, via two GEC traction motors. The saloon car layout had good all-round visibility for the passengers, and sliding access bodyside doors were fitted.

The English Electric Co built a very similar railcar at its Dick Kerr Preston works in 1933 but with a less powerful 200hp EECo engine. This was called *Bluebird* and ran trials on the LMSR. It was nearly 70ft long (exceptional for the period) and had the capacity to haul a trailer. Compared to the Armstrong Whitworth cars it was somewhat under-powered and seems — as in so many other cases — to have faded quietly away from the public eye.

Although in North America, and elsewhere, there was a steady development of the diesel-electric passenger train in the late 1930s, the interest in Britain seems to have dwindled, and only the GWR AEC diesel-mechanicals kept the flag flying for the diesel railcar on the home railways; although firms such as English Electric and Armstrong Whitworth were fully aware of the potential of the export market. The outbreak of World War 2 temporarily halted any further progress which might have been forthcoming, and the immediate postwar years, with oil-fuel rationing in Britain, were not very conducive to a resumption of diesel-electric railcar development. Thus the idea lay almost dormant in Great Britain from the mid-1930s until the early 1950s, when some revival of interest was expressed, in a report prepared for the British Transport Commission (BTC) which recommended the use of diesel-electric railcars on parts of the Southern Region that were still steam operated; in particular on cross-country routes in Hampshire. Nothing came of this first report to the BTC, but the recommendation was evidently remembered when the vast Modernisation Plan was being drawn up, as we shall see later.

In Part 8 I have described how the scheme for the introduction of diesel-mechanical railcars was in fact, approved *before* the 1955 BTC Modernisation Plan, and how it was one aspect of the strategy for future traction produced by R. A. Riddles and his team of BR engineers. When Riddles envisaged the use of railcars it was as an alternative to his real desire, which was to electrify virtually the whole rail system; phasing out steam stage by stage. Riddles had recognised the role of the diesel in shunting duties, and he thought that lightweight railbuses could be used on some branch lines, and on some local services. Later on he reluctantly realised that the diesel might have to provide a more important 'stop-gap' between steam and electric operation, due to lack of available finance and manufacturing capacity; which meant that electrification was going to be a relatively long-term achievement. The diesel-mechanical railcars were therefore justifiable in the fairly short term — although in fact they have in many cases had to last a good deal longer than was envisaged at the time; 20 years being thought of as their maximum lifespan when first authorised.

On the Southern Region the diesel-mechanicals were *outlawed* from the start, and when the BTC Modernisation Plan allocated the SR a quota of routes to be dieselised, there was never any question that these would involve the use of diesel-mechanicals. It was necessary to introduce diesel railcars in order to end the use of steam as soon as possible, (before electrification could be introduced) because the SR possessed at that time rather more than its fair share of vintage steam locomotives and rolling stock, in use on numerous branch lines and secondary lines; despite an infusion of new LMR-type steam locomotives in the early 1950s — the Fairburn Class 4 2-6-4T and the Ivatt Class 2 2-6-2T. In country areas push-pull motor-trains were often still the mainstay of passenger services; worked by a variety of pre-Grouping tank engines. For these routes, and for two more important routes not yet scheduled for electrification, a quantity of diesel railcars would be necessary; including some of main line, or inter-city, category for the London-Tunbridge Wells-Hastings services. These railcars were to be of the diesel-electric type, and therefore did not adhere to the lightweight specification of the diesel mechanicals.

The basic reasoning behind the adoption of diesel-electric transmission for the SR was unquestionably sound. With a wealth of electric traction experience, and with fully trained staff, the electric generator and traction motors did not hold the mysteries for the SR men that they would have presented on the Western or Scottish Regions for example! Furthermore, a very reliable and suitable diesel engine already existed, in use in shunting locomotives; in the form of the English Electric Co type 4SRKT 500hp engine. This four cylinder engine was a smaller version of the 16-cylinder 10in bore EE Co engine used in the pioneer LMSR diesel-electric Co-Co No 10000 of 1,600hp (See part 1 of this series). English Electric had already supplied both versions to the Egyptian State Railways in 1947, in a contract which included some five-car diesel-electric passenger trains fitted with the four-cylinder version; known as the 4SRKT; the

Left:
A very typical scene, with two 'Hampshire' three-car DEMUs at Alresford station on 29 November 1969, with units Nos 1128, on a down train, and 1122 on an up Alton-bound train. The signalman was about to change the single line token from one train to the other; Alresford then being the only passing place, or station with a signalbox on the route, by that date. Both DEMUs are in BR blue livery, with full yellow ends, and both have the engine compartment and brakevan nearest the camera; hence the inverted black triangles. *John A. M. Vaughan*

Below:
East Sussex, or 'Oxted' three-car unit No 1309 is seen leaving Tunbridge Wells West on a mid-afternoon working to East Grinstead — a route closed by Dr Beeching. From East Grinstead the train worked forward to London, Victoria. The 'Oxted' sets feature a more attractive front end design fabricated in moulded glass fibre. The unit is in original green livery. On the left, two of Riddles' BR standard Class 4 2-6-4Ts bask in the sun outside the engine shed. The DEMUs displaced these modern steam engines on the Southern Region. *D. F. Chipchase*

larger version being the 16 SVT. The SR took the above mentioned Egyptian design as their starting point, and two engines of 500hp each were placed one each end of a six-car layout (Hastings units) or one engine only, at one end of a three-car layout (Hampshire and Oxted units). The main generator was an English Electric EE824/26 and current was fed to two standard SR type EE507 traction motors. These traction motors were installed in the *rear* bogie of each power car, under the passenger accommodation, in order to keep the axle load down on the leading bogie, which had the engine and generator above it.

A marriage of the bulky EE Co engine and generator mounted *above* floor level in a special compartment, to the standard axle-mounted traction motors of SR electric stock produced a simple and effective self-contained diesel powered railcar. However the word railcar was really a misnomer, because the SR chose to build heavyweight steel-bodied units, using the same jigs and components as had been produced for their contemporary electric multiple-unit stock; which was directly based upon the standard BR Mk 1 design, with steel underframe to full main line specification. (A variation in design was required for the Hastings line stock, of which more anon). Not only did the SR produce trains to existing standards of construction, it also chose to produce trains to existing standards of design; in terms of appearance and passenger comfort. In other words, the 1951 Standard carriage — already becoming somewhat out-moded in style — was simply motorised, and produced in sufficient quantities to form a diesel-electric multiple unit fleet. No doubt very considerable savings in cost were achieved by this practice, but it succeeded in presenting the public with a fleet of trains which showed no visible improvement upon the most recent stock, the 1951 designs produced for haulage by steam, or worked by electricity! It was a poor public relations exercise, and not at all in the prevailing spirit of the time, as motivated by the BTC. As pieces of machinery they have been very successful, but as a mode of conveyance they have kept the passenger firmly back in the final days of steam-orientated thinking in terms of aesthetics and amenity design.

If these words seem a little harsh, it is simply because they emphasise the 'Ivory tower' attitude that prevailed on the SR at that time. Whereas the designers of the diesel-mechanical railcars went to great lengths to produce a new passenger environment, with pleasing views from the windows, and reasonable seating, toilet facilities, and in the majority of cases inter-carriage gangways, and had also tried to provide a pleasing external styling; the SR made no concessions in this manner whatsoever, even relegating a single toilet facility to the centre trailer of the *non-gangwayed* three-car sets in the case of the Oxted line units — shades of the pre-Grouping days! But the horror-of-horrors of the BR Modernisation Plan were the Hastings line units, produced in order to bring about a quick improvement to an ailing steam-worked service, which was low on the electrification priority list. The line was hampered by some loading gauge restrictions in particular in certain tunnels, which had meant using special narrow-bodied carriages in steam days, when the 'Schools' class 4-4-0s were the largest express passenger power cleared to work the line.

At the time of Nationalisation, the Hastings services were experiencing increased patronage, and the heavy loads were beginning to tell upon the 'Schools'. Also the rolling stock was in poor physical shape from the passenger's viewpoint, and a scheme was implemented to build new locomotive-hauled carriages of specially modified Mk 1 type, with 9ft 0in wide flat sided bodies, and a shorter than standard underframe of 58ft 0in. In 1955 construction of a batch of 32 new coaches was underway at Eastleigh for the replacement of some of the existing locomotive-hauled stock. When the decision was taken to dieselise the line, these carriages were earmarked for completion as the trailers and power cars for seven six-car diesel-electric sets; to commence working the more important business services in the 1957 summer timetable. Thus much of the design work was already complete *before* the decision to dieselise, and the modification to produce the required power cars was the only major change in design required. No one seems to have given any thought to the possibility — surely there — of redesigning the spartan 1951-style interiors, or of producing a smart and stylish exterior to herald the new Modernisation Plan! What appeared from Eastleigh was perhaps the most drab flat-faced, flat-sided 'box-on-wheels' ever to run on British Railways! *Gone* was the flair and imagination which had produced the prewar AEC railcars, or the LMSR 1938 articulated set, for example, and in its place was a utilitarian run-about; which proved to be rather bad-riding into the bargain!

Further Hastings units were subsequently ordered to the *same* design, but with longer underframes of 63ft 5in, (why, one wonders had 58ft 0in been considered necessary before?) and these completed the scheme. Mechanically the Hastings units have performed well, and were a credit to St Leonards depot where they were based, but what a pity they were so

Below:
To date only one Southern Region DEMU has received a complete refurbishment, although it is still possible that some more will follow in order to keep them fit for the Uckfield shuttle service that is planned. 'Hampshire' set No 1111 (note the numbers over both windows) received internal design changes, including gangways between vehicles within the set, and the exterior was painted in full BR blue and grey livery. It is seen at Rye on an Ashford-Hastings train on 12 July 1980.
P. A. Brown

poorly designed from the public's viewpoint. Happily the riding qualities were somewhat improved after they were first built, and the EE Co engines gave stalwart performance, but the flat sided steel bodies had very severe corrosion problems in recent years. One latterday improvement of a minor nature was the substitution of BR two-tone blue and grey livery with full yellow ends instead of the previous drab blue overall, and original SR green overall, both of which had somehow emphasised their boxlike bodies.

The other diesel units required by the SR were mainly for cross-country routes or outer-suburban services. These were closely based upon the then standard 2-HAP electric units although the need to place the engine and generator above floor level meant a reduction in passenger accommodation. The addition of a new trailer to make up three-car sets became necessary, due to overcrowding, and some more three-car sets were delivered new as such, as is described in the relevant Sections.

For the Oxted line a special batch of 19 three-car sets had to be built with narrower bodies for clearance reasons (not, however, flat-sided) and these were the last to appear under the Modernisation Plan orders for the SR. On these sets an attempt was at last made to produce a more pleasing front end, and a somewhat brighter interior decor, but the same basic layout was adhered to, and like their Hastings cousins they were rough-riding.

In fact the Oxted sets were the only SR diesel units to receive any BR Design Panel treatment, but some of the later diesel-mechanical designs had the benefit of industrial design advice, as is related in Part 8 of this *British Rail Fleet Survey* series. The Design Panel was not established at the time the bulk of the production design was underway and a good many railcars were built to the individual tastes of the various outside manufacturers; not always with the happiest of results! Indeed, BR itself produced one of the poorest front end designs (at Swindon of all places!) for the Edinburgh-Glasgow inter-city sets; having apparently forgotten the GWR example of earlier days. It was in fact adverse public reaction to these Swindon railcars, and to the Hastings units, that convinced the BTC of the need to establish proper design standards for its new trains; hence the creation of the Design Panel in August 1956, a story I have fully covered in my book *BR 1948-1983 A Journey by Design*; published by Ian Allan Ltd.

On the brighter side was the superior heating in the SR DEMUs, by electricity, made possible by their power equipment, and the sturdier construction of the seats and luggage racks, which meant that SR travellers were spared the oily heat and constant vibrations that soon became two of the less attractive features of the diesel-mechanicals used on the other Regions. Sad to relate, the diesel engines were themselves noisy, and conversation, or train announcements on station platforms were frequently obliterated by the English Electric 'roar', even when the train was stationary. Once on the move the SR DEMUs had good acceleration, and vastly superior brakes when compared to their DMU counterparts. If only more attention had been paid to their passenger interiors and external appearance!

A solitary SR three-car diesel-electric *was* (in 1979) internally refurbished as an experiment, but no further vehicles have been treated at the time of writing, and it seems likely that many of these units will be displaced by electrification schemes, or perhaps by new 'Sprinter' DMUs, in a fairly short-term strategy; although some may be given heavy overhauls for the Oxted-Uckfield line. The one refurbished set, No 1111 had gangways added between carriages, but not at the driving ends, and a much brighter interior decor, with fluorescent lighting — showing what could have been done right at the beginning, if more enlightened designers had been at the Eastleigh drawing boards.

Mention must be made of one experiment that took place in 1956, because had it been successful, it might have changed the future face of the BR diesel railcar fleet. The idea of an underfloor mounted diesel-electric power unit, giving more

Below:
The final years of the 'Hastings' units saw them in BR blue and grey livery. No 1035, minus buffet car, enters Wadhurst station on 17 October 1983 en route to Hastings. The long-awaited electrification has eliminated the need to find replacement DEMUs on this busy route. *John Gofts*

Below:
Created from two LMSR 1928 all-steel open brake seconds, at Derby, the Paxman diesel-electric set ran extensive trials on BR. Paxman ZHXL 450hp engines were under-floor mounted, and the motor bogies were secondhand from Euston-Watford electric stock. The train never ran in passenger service. *GEC Diesels Ltd*

Bottom:
An opportunity missed on BR was the use of Mk 2 DEMUs; the design actually having been prepared and constructed for service in Northern Ireland. This unit, No 99, is named *Sir Myles Humphreys*, with the small nameplate just behind the driver's door. *Rory J. Semple*

space for passengers in the carriage, and allowing the provision of through gangways between sets (a feature not possible on the SR diesel-electrics with their engines above underframe level) and giving considerably more power than the road-vehicle type diesel engine of the mechanical railcars could provide, held considerable appeal. It would allow railcars to be used on fast inter-city routes, with power to cope with the loads and the gradients similar to that provided by locomotives — whilst offering the quick turnround abilities of railcars. Suitable routes, in the planner's eyes were Liverpool-Leeds and Brighton/Portsmouth-Bristol-Cardiff, in particular. Taking the Liverpool-Leeds route, the Derby engineers from both the carriage and wagon and the mechanical departments, worked together to produce a prototype two-car set utilising existing carriages and parts to save initial costs of development. The engines, however, were new and of Paxman design.

The Paxman 6-cylinder 6ZHXL flat engine developed 450hp and could be accommodated under the floor, coupled to a BTH generator, with power going to one bogie on each car. (The bogies used were from redundant LMR Euston-Watford EMU stock.) The Paxman engine had already been tried out in the very experimental 'Fell' diesel locomotive, built at Derby. The carriage bodies were two ex-LMSR 1926-built all-steel open brake seconds with driving cabs adapted to the outer ends; forming a mobile test bed. The unit, which never ran in public service, was liveried in the standard railcar dark green, with cream lining and 'speed whiskers' on the ends. Trials were conducted at high speeds between Derby and St Pancras; Euston and Rugby; Derby and Gloucester, and then on the ER between Sheffield and York and London King's Cross. Finally, a daily series of trials took place over the difficult Derby-Carlisle route. Although some 43,000 miles were thus covered in 17 months the Derby authorities declined the new design on the basis that the equipment was too expensive and too heavy. (The two-car set weighed 103 tons.) The Paxman engine was later adopted for the twin-engined Type 1 Bo-Bo locomotives of Class 17, described in Part 4 of this series.

In the early 1960s the idea of a through Brighton-Cardiff railcar service was once again considered, using 900hp four-car DEMU sets capable of working in multiple. The Paxman engine already mentioned was again evaluated, but alternatives were now available in the form of the Dorman 12-cylinder 12QT type (tried out in 'Hampshire' unit No 1129, as described in Section 2); the underfloor AEC engine rated at 230hp (two per two power cars), and the six-cylinder version of the EE Co RKT. (The latter being established as too heavy.) The project was stillborn, but the 230hp underfloor engine did materialise in some Swindon-built inter-city sets, as described in Part 8 of this series.

A further word on liveries. In recent years all the SR DEMUs have run in standard blue and grey livery; a scheme which has certainly brightened up their appearance somewhat. When new, the sets were in plain green (a slightly darker and more yellow shade than SR malachite — which they never carried) and the roof area was medium grey. The bogies, underframes and associated underbody equipment were painted black. Standard Gill Sans lettering and numerals were applied in cream transfers, edged by a fine black line. No lining-out was considered necessary, and the front bufferbeam area was black, never red. In these respects the DEMUs closely resembled their EMU counterparts — only the noises were different! When the BR corporate identity scheme was introduced, the DEMUs were given a plain rail blue livery; at first with a dismal matt paint finish. Prior to this some carried yellow warning panels on the front ends, and an early experiment had involved the application of a fluorescent orange 'vee' (V) on at least one Hampshire area unit. This was to alert station staff at which end to load and unload the luggage van, as the train was approching the platform. When the yellow panels and then the yellow warning ends were applied, a black inverted triangle was painted on instead to make the same advance staff warning. Note that only one end of each unit had brakevan/luggage accommodation, except the Hastings main line sets. Final, and present-day, livery is standard blue and grey.

With the Hastings line electrification having finally commenced operation in May 1986, and with approval given for the electrification of the East Grinstead line in the summer of 1985 (for completion by the end of 1987) it is clear that the SR DEMU fleet will soon be considerably diminished; in particular by withdrawal of the Hastings units for scrap, and then by displacement of the 'Oxted' sets; although some of the latter may work the proposed Oxted-Uckfield shuttle service. The situation is further complicated by the obligation — following an agreement between the British Railways Board (BRB) and the railway trade unions — to withdraw *all* passenger vehicles containing blue asbestos insulation by the end of 1987; unless they have had the asbestos removed. Significantly, Swindon Works continued to remove asbestos from SR DEMUs (the 'Hampshire' and 'Oxted' sets) *after* all such work was cancelled for diesel-mechanical railcars. It therefore appears that *some* life-extension may take place, if only as a stop-gap until new 'Sprinter' units or more electrification, can replace them.

Finally, it would be less than polite to ignore 'the ones that got away'; so conveniently overlooked by many BR commentators! I refer to the subsequent development of the SR DEMU, using the integral Mk 2 body and the vastly superior B4/5 bogies; whilst retaining the same basic power equipment layout. This logical, and desirable development never took to the BR metals, which is a great pity because it offered a much improved product from the passenger's viewpoint. It was, however, built in some numbers, and shipped in conditions of some secrecy (for security reasons) from Derby Works to the Northern Ireland Railways, where the design has given much satisfaction. A thousand pities that prevailing attitudes prevented its adoption as a BR standard — as will be related further on. Instead, all the SR DEMUs date from the BR Mk 1 period and are dated in terms of bogie design and passenger amenities. However, what they have lacked in these respects has been more then recompensed by their abilities for hard work and their reliability when compared to some of their diesel-mechanical cousins of similar vintage.

A general note about the presentation of this volume is necessary. It falls into three main parts, each with its own introduction, but the presentation of each Section remains constant, and to the series style. Each design is dealt with in chronological order, by date of original entry into service; or date of rebuilding or reformation, in the case of some hybrid SR DEMUs.

Space does not permit lists of individual vehicle numbers and readers are advised that such lists and details of depot allocations can be found in the Ian Allan *abc British Rail Multiple-units*, published each year. The diesel-electric 'Blue Pullman' trains, the prototype, and the production series of High Speed Trains (HSTs) are not included in this volume. Readers will find full coverage of these express passenger diesel-electric units in Part 5 of this series, entitled *High Speed Trains*.

The drawings by David Gibbons of British Rail first appeared in the official newspaper of BR, *Rail News*, and the author expresses his gratitude for their inclusion in this volume. Readers will be interested to know that a book of David Gibbons' remarkable work has recently been published by Ian Allan Ltd. My sincere thanks also to James Abbott and Roger Ford of *Modern Railways* for the extracts taken from that highly-informed and perceptive journal. I often think it should be made compulsory reading in all BR offices — but that's another story!

Once again, the author wishes to thank Messrs A. B. MacLeod and S. W. Stevens-Stratten of the Ian Allan Library for much assistance and Colin Marsden and Alec Swain for photographic selections which filled some gaps during the compilation of this, the ninth book in the *British Rail Fleet Survey* series. Finally, my thanks to the many railwaymen and enthusiasts who have helped in various ways since the series began in 1981.

Brian Haresnape FRSA, NDD
Gassin, Saint Tropez, France
May 1986

The Southern DEMUs

The entire SR DEMU fleet dates from the BTC's ambitious Modernisation Plan era, and was constructed between 1957 and 1962, to basic Mk 1 standards but with loading gauge modifications in some cases.

A high degree of standardisation was made possible by utilising one type of well-proven diesel engine, and an existing traction motor type used in SR electric multiple-units.

Below:
'Hastings' set No 1003 posed for the official publicity pictures, taken in February 1957, before the new service was introduced. The plain livery, devoid of lining-out, and the slab sides and very basic front end design were typical of Eastleigh's lack of attention to aesthetic details. Note the large headcode numerals originally carried and the buckeye coupling in the dropped position. Note also the whistle placed horizontally above the driver's window. *British Railways*

1 Eastleigh Works, BR. Main Line Services 6-Car. Class 201/2/3 (SR Class 6S/6L/5L)

Introduced: 1957/58*
Purpose: London-Hastings main line services, via Tonbridge
No of Cars per unit: 6/5†
TOPS Class: 201/2*/3*
Engines: English Electric Co 4SRKT
Horsepower: 1,000
Transmission: Electrical. Two nose-suspended axle-hung traction motors
Body: 58ft 0in × 9ft 0in/64ft 6in × 9ft 0in*
Units Nos: 1001-1007/1011-1032*/1034-1037*†
Brake Type: Auto-air/Electro-pneumatic
Maximum speed: 90mph
Coupling restrictions: Within SR diesel-electric MU types only
Original Running Nos/Vehicle Type/Weight: S60000-S60009/S60010-S60031*/S60032-S60045*†, DMBS, 54tons 2cwt/55 tons*†. S60500-S60520/S60521-S60547*/S60548/S60561*†, TS, 29 tons/30 tons*†. S60700-S60706/S60707-S60715*/S60716-S60722*†, TF(K). 30 tons/31 tons*†. S60750-S60756*†, TB, 35 tons*†.

Notes: *indicates long underframe type. †indicates long underframe type with trailer Buffet car. In 1980 the Buffet cars were removed, and the 5L units were formed from the Class 203 (6B) units; having only five cars per set.

I have already described the genesis of the 'Hastings' DEMU design in the Introduction. Ordered in April 1955, the first units were needed for the 1957 summer service, and in fact the first unit, six-car set No 1001 was completed at Eastleigh in February 1957 and ran an initial trial between Waterloo and Bournemouth Central, covering the 111½ miles in 120 minutes, including a three-minute stop at Southampton.

The first seven sets were on the 56ft 11in underframes (with 58ft 0in bodies) originally ordered for locomotive-hauled carriages. These were insufficient to allow the complete Hastings service to be dieselised, and a further 16 six-car sets were authorised. By this time someone had done their homework properly and it was realised that the standard BR Mk 1 underframe of 63ft 5in could be used on the route, provided that the 64ft 6in overall carriage *body* was kept to the same narrow flat-sided design of the first seven sets. The final seven sets on the longer underframes each included a Buffet car. A feature of the first class accommodation was that it was in compartments with side access doors to each, whereas the second class was all in the open saloon type layout. The full diesel service went into operation on 9 June 1958, and until May 1986, the line was worked exclusively by these sets from that day. Their versatility has also made them popular with SR operators for use elsewhere on the Region, and on other regions for special excursion work; particularly at weekends when there were spare sets available.

Some teething troubles were encountered, in particular with noisy power units and poor riding, particularly the powered bogies. The noise was caused by the turbocharger which had a distinct and high-pitched whistling sound, and a silencer had to be fitted, following numerous public objections, mostly from lineside dwellers. The bogies were eventually modified but it cannot be said that the quality of ride ever equalled that provided by the later designs such as the B4/B5 type. Once initial problems had been overcome, the units settled down to give very reliable service, and it is only in their final days that it proved difficult to keep them up to

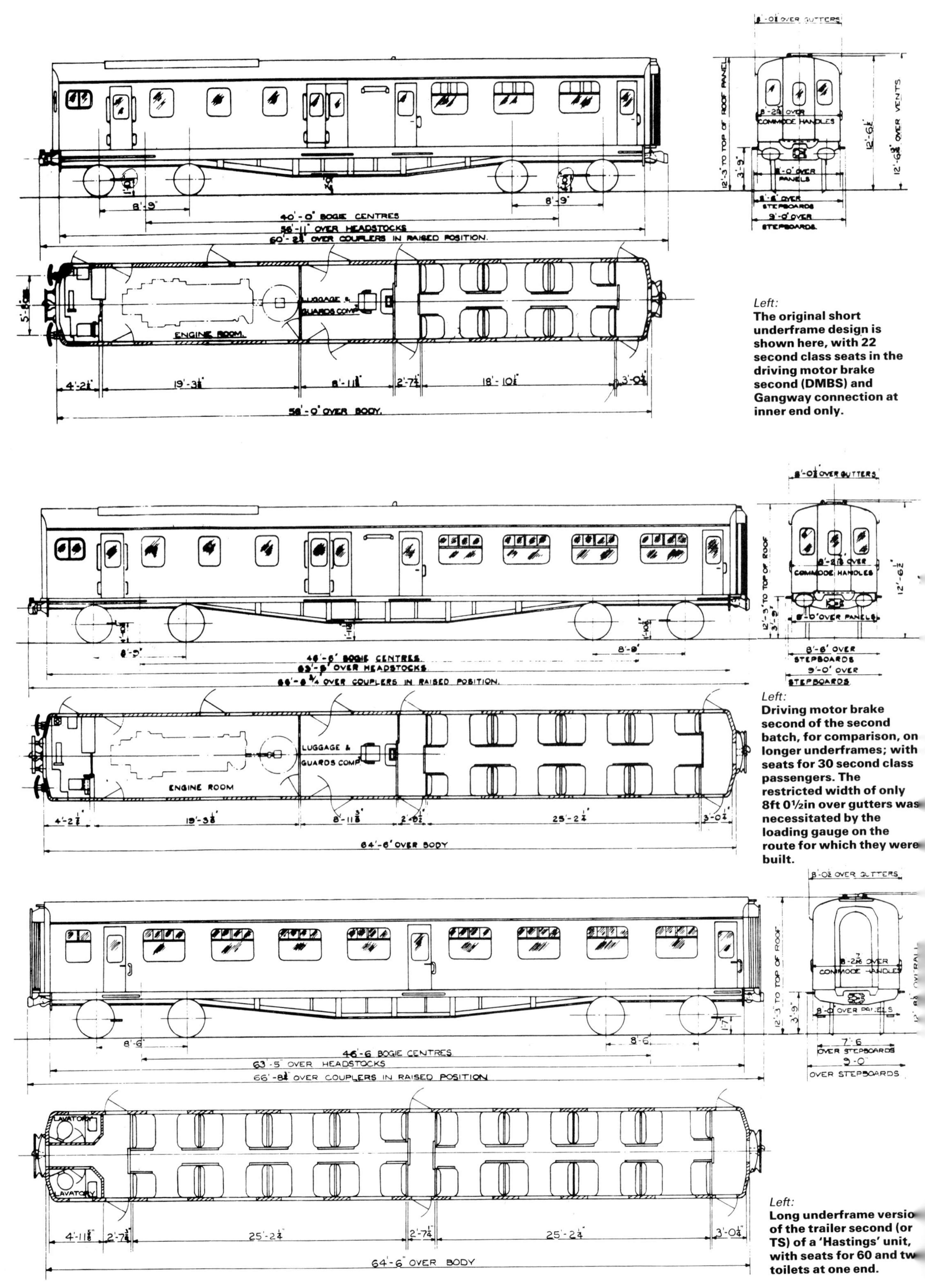

Left:
The original short underframe design is shown here, with 22 second class seats in the driving motor brake second (DMBS) and Gangway connection at inner end only.

Left:
Driving motor brake second of the second batch, for comparison, on longer underframes; with seats for 30 second class passengers. The restricted width of only 8ft 0½in over gutters was necessitated by the loading gauge on the route for which they were built.

Left:
Long underframe versio of the trailer second (or TS) of a 'Hastings' unit, with seats for 60 and tw toilets at one end.

scratch, with the result that mixed formations of power cars from different units became increasingly common.

The introduction of the new units stimulated passenger traffic, which increased by some 40% in the first few years of operation, and what they lacked in glamour and comfort was compensated for by fast, regular services and punctuality (the latter feature had been sadly lacking in the last years of steam). A special shed was constructed at St Leonards to service the units. The proximity of this shed to the seashore was to prove a problem, because constant exposure to sea air created serious corrosion of the carriages' steel body panels over the years, and much patching/welding became necessary to keep the units presentable.

Three of the original short underframe units were withdrawn in 1964 and the vehicles disbanded. The six power cars and some trailers were then utilised in six three-car hybrid sets for the Tonbridge-Redhill-Reading service. These sets, which became known as the 'Tadpoles' are fully described in Section 4. These power cars were returned to the Hastings service when the 'Tadpoles' were disbanded in 1979-1981. In 1976 the buffet cars were removed from two sets and one was subsequently converted to become the SR General Manager's saloon No TDB 975025. The other suffered a remarkable rebuilding at Derby, where it was mounted upon experimental APT bogies and used as a tilt testing car — being suitable on account of the narrow body width. The remaining buffet cars were all withdrawn from service in 1980, due to declining patronage and increasing costs of staffing and operation.

During the 1960s the English Electric Co decided to cease production of the four-cylinder engine, and this created a problem for the SR by making spare parts difficult or costly to obtain. Fortunately the Ministry of Defence had purchased some SRKT engines for use as standby generator sets. These had hardly been used when the SR was able to purchase them second-hand as a source of spares and replacements.

It was perhaps an unfortunate publicity idea to put red stickers on the sides of the power cars in their twilight days with the slogan 'Ride the 1066 Route'. Passengers may well have gained the impression that it referred to the condition of the bodywork of the stock — a factor alone which would have made rapid replacement necessary! Happily the decision was at last taken to electrify the route and improve the tunnel loading gauge clearances. The hard-worked Hastings DEMUs were displaced from the London-Hastings route with the introduction of the new electrified service with the summer timetable in May 1986. However, despite the anticipated withdrawal of all the 'Hastings' units with the end of their traditional duties, a number of units, some reduced in number of trailer vehicles, were retained in use to cover a shortage of DEMU sets on other Southern Region services.

Below:
Long underframe set No 1034, with buffet car (fourth vehicle) departs from Crowhurst, soon after delivery from Eastleigh. Note the oil lamp carried on the rear end, and buckeye coupling in raised position. *P. J. Sharpe*

Left:
The trailer first design featured compartments and side corridor, and there were bodyside access doors to every compartment. This is the trailer first of set No 1019, on long underframe, with eight compartments and two toilets. The corridor side had only four access doors spaced, with windows between. *P. J. Sharpe*

Right:
The buffet car of 'Hastings' set No 1036, in plain green SR livery, at Tonbridge. The passengers were placed over the bogies and a rough ride was liable to produce considerable spillage of tea, coffee and stronger beverages. *Brian Haresnape*

Above:
After a period when plain BR blue livery was applied, the welcome decision to give the 'Hastings' sets full blue and grey was taken. It brightened up their dull contours to some good effect! Sporting the new colours, complete with yellow warning ends, set No 1011 is seen in sylvan spring surroundings as it climbs Hildenborough bank on the 11.43 Hastings-Charing Cross working on 12 May 1973. A second unit is at the rear, to form a typical 12-car train. Lack of front end gangways meant that passengers could not pass from one set to another; effectively isolating the buffet car facilities from one half of a 12-car payload! The original whistle was replaced by two roof-mounted air horns on all SR DEMUs. *Brian Morrison*

Right:
An unusual use for two 'Hastings' power cars was to work the BRB Track Testing Car No DB999550 on 30 May 1985. Two Class 201 (6S) driving cars sandwiched the test vehicle, and the difference in body widths was very evident in this photograph taken at New Malden. The special ran from Stewarts Lane to Weymouth and back. *Colin J. Marsden*

Top:

When the Redhill-Reading 'Tadpoles' were disbanded (see Section four) the motor coaches went back to the Hastings line, to create a pool of spares. Hence this rare view of a short underframe motor coach (still in plain blue livery, and carrying 'Tadpole' set No 1204) at the head of a long-underframe unit, complete with Buffet car. Photographed near Elmstead Woods on the 13.40 Charing Cross-Hastings working on 22 August 1974. *Brian Morrison*

Above:

For five years the 'Hastings' units were responsible for the Saturdays-only Brighton-Exeter train, until replaced by locomotives and stock from May 1977. This interesting working took them far from their usual area of operation. Units Nos 1034 and 1035 leave Salisbury with the return working on 2 April 1977. *G. F. Gillham*

Left:

Driving motor brake second No S60045 from Class 203 unit No 1037 stands outside St Leonards depot, home for the 'Hastings' units until their demise in May 1986. *BR Southern Region*

Right:
The first of the 'Hastings' DEMUs to be withdrawn was Class 202 No 1019. DMBS No 60030 sheds a tear outside its home depot at St Leonards on 15 June 1985.
T. J. Saunders

Below:
When the Buffet cars were withdrawn from service, the vehicles became redundant, and one, No S60755 was rebuilt completely to become the SR General Manager's Saloon; No TDB975025. It is fully equipped for push-pull working, and has a powerful headlamp for tunnel inspection. This vehicle was included in the Royal Train on the occasion of the wedding of Prince Charles and Lady Diana Spencer. *J. G. Glover*

Right:
BR Research and Development (R&D) Department vehicle No RDB975386 Lab No 4 *Hastings*. This is a former Hastings line buffet car, No S60750, rebuilt for experiments associated with the Advanced Passenger Train (APT) project. It is mounted on modified R&D bogies, with tilt facility — the narrow body making it suitable for such use. Bar couplings with no side buffers are fitted and the maximum speed is 110mph — rather more than it ever experienced in SR service!
Colin J. Marsden

2 Eastleigh Works, BR. Branch Line & Local Services 2/3-Car. Class 205 (SR Class 3H)

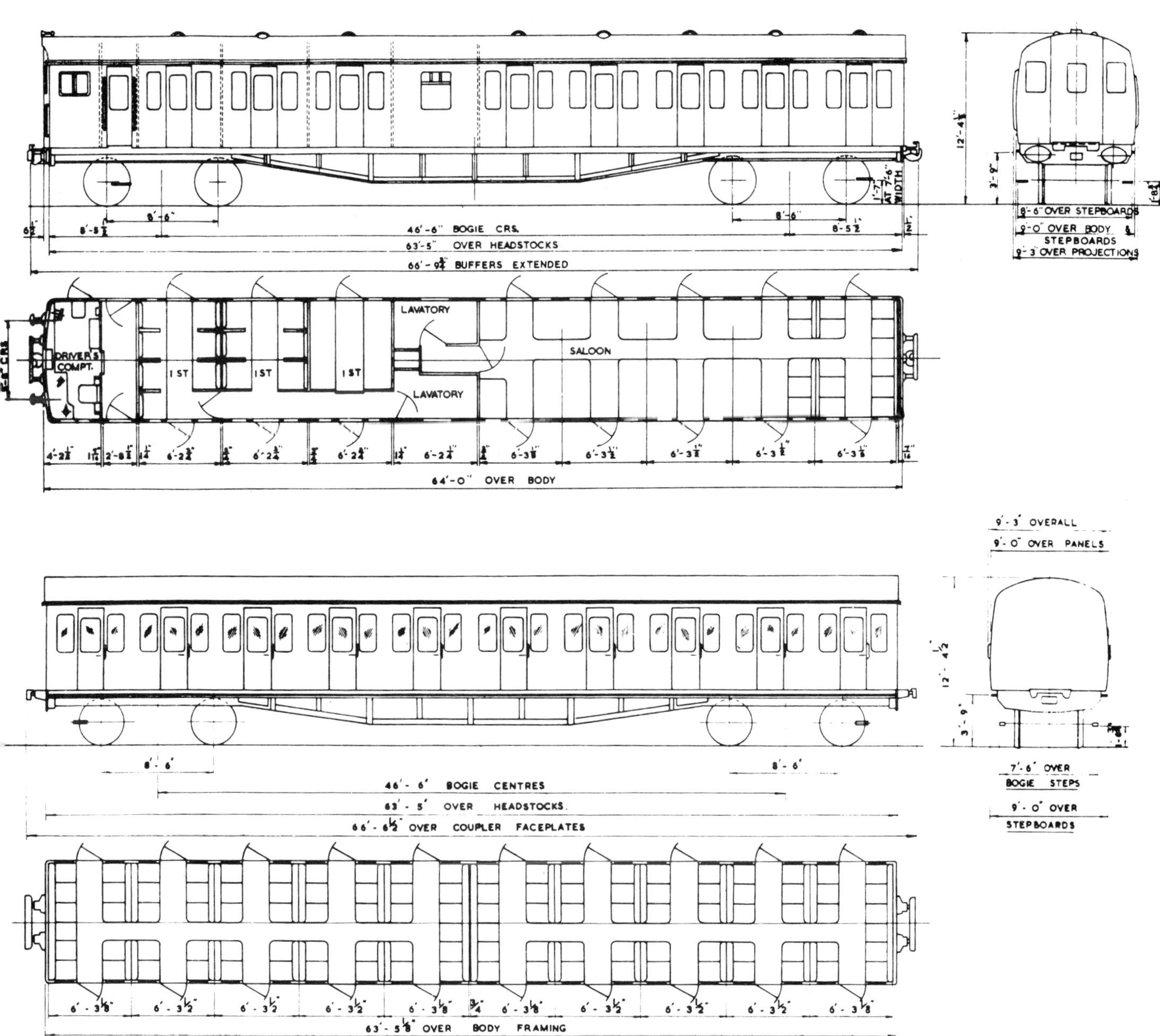

Introduced: 1957
Purpose: Branch line and local services in non-electrified SR areas
No of Cars per unit: 2*/3
TOPS Class: 205
Engine: English Electric Co 4SRKT
Horsepower: 600
Transmission; Electrical. Two nose-suspended axle-hung traction motors
Body: 64ft×9ft 3in/63ft 6in×9ft 3in†
Unit Nos: 1101-1133
Brake Type: Auto-air/Electro-pneumatic
Maximum speed: 75mph
Coupling restrictions: Within SR diesel-electric MU types only; except unit No 1111 which can couple with certain electric MUs on the SR.
Original running Nos/Vehicle type/Weight: S60100-S60125, DMBS, 56 tons. S60650-S60671, TS, 31 tons*†. S77500/3/7/8, TS, 30 tons*†. S60800-S60825, DTC, 32 tons.

Notes: *Unit Nos 1101-1118 ran originally as two-car sets and then had new trailer seconds inserted. Units 1119-1122 ran longer as two-car sets and then had secondhand trailer seconds (less seats) inserted. Unit No 1111 has been refurbished and reclassified as 3H (M). It has no first class accommodation; the former DTC becoming a DTS.
†Trailer seconds are 63ft 6in in length.

The Southern Region possessed a considerable network of country branch lines prior to the Beeching slaughter. The

Top:
The drawing shows a driving trailer composite (DTC) of a Class 205 'Hampshire' unit, with two lavatories in the centre of the vehicle to serve first class and second class accommodation. No gangways are fitted to inner end of the trailer, thus restricting access to the toilet to a single carriage — a strangely Victorian attitude to life! The East Sussex-based units have three first class compartments, as shown here, whereas the Eastleigh-based 'Hampshires' have the compartment nearest the driver as second class accommodation. Another alternative has this end compartment in use as luggage space.

Above:
No less than 104 second class seats were available in the centre trailer second — but no gangway ends to allow these luckless passengers access to the toilets!

Right:
Set No 1121, actually one of the four built for service in East Sussex, nevertheless typifies the original appearance of the two-car 'Hampshire' DEMUs. Features to note are the whistle above the driver's window, and the large numerals in the headcode panel. Plain SR green livery was carried, with Gill Sans lettering and numerals. Set No 1121 was photographed entering Appledore on the 2.40pm Ashford-Hastings train on 21 February 1961. *M. Edwards*

Below:
An additional trailer was inserted in the middle of the two-car sets to augment their accommodation, following problems with overcrowding. The engine horsepower was increased to 600hp to cope with the added load (see text for details). In plain green livery, set No 1115 stands in a siding at Three Bridges on 30 October 1966. The large 'vee' was in fluorescent orange paint, and denoted the end of the unit which had the brake compartment — to alert station staff who had to load or unload quickly. *Alec Swain*

Bottom:
When the first small yellow warning panels were applied to EMUs and DEMUs on the SR, the orange 'vee' was replaced by an inverted black triangle, as seen here on set No 1111 at Basingstoke on 20 June 1965; evidently fresh from a repaint in SR green at Eastleigh. There are now smaller numerals in the route indicator box, and the whistle has been replaced by two roof-mounted air horns. *Alec Swain*

majority of them were worked by steam locomotives (often on push and pull trains) and these locomotives and carriages were of considerable vintage in some cases. Before leaving the SR, the last CME, Mr Oliver Bulleid had designed his revolutionary 0-6-6-0T 'Leader' class steam design with a view to using it on such services, to bring them up-to-date until such a time as electrification was possible. The 'Leader' proved to be an abject failure and the construction order was cancelled after only one had even been completed and steamed, with the result that the old engines had to soldier on for a few more years. When the BTC Modernisation Plan was announced it included the provision, first recommended in a 1951 report to the BTC — known as the Bowles report — for diesel-electric railcars to replace steam on these SR branch lines; commencing in the Hampshire area. A batch of 18 two-car units was ordered for construction at Eastleigh, and these were each to be fitted with one four-cylinder 500hp engine of the same type as in the Hastings units, and to use the same standard SR traction motors.

What Eastleigh produced was basically a diesel-electric powered version of the 2-HAP electric multiple-unit, with standard Mk 1 body and underframe; without the loading gauge restriction that the Hastings design had required. The power car had second class seating in an open saloon layout with slam doors to each bay. The trailer had the first class seating arranged in side corridor compartment style, each with side doors. Toilets were provided in the trailer, but not in the power car, and there was no gangway connection between the two, thereby restricting access to the toilets, whilst the train was moving, only to passengers in the trailer car. Interior design and furnishing

Above:
Comparison with the two preceding illustrations shows the difference on the two sides of the engine room compartment. Three fixed windows are spaced along the side opposite that carrying the radiator louvres and access door, as can be seen in this view of set No 1110 at Bealieu Road, heading for Southampton on 18 June 1966. *Alec Swain*

Left:
One of the first SR units to be repainted in BR blue livery was DEMU No 1103, done at Eastleigh, and seen here on 12 July 1966. The paint at first used had a curious matt finish and soon became unattractive. A small yellow warning panel (no black triangle on the driving trailer end, of course) white numerals and symbol and deep umber brown bogies and underframe, were other features of the new livery as first introduced. The compartment nearest the driver carries the label 'luggage' on the door, next to it is the first class portion of the set. *John H. Bird*

was to BR 1951-style standards and no concessions in design were made to give passengers a better view, in particular at the front ends — a feature very popular with the contemporary diesel-mechanical railcars being introduced on the other Regions. A plain green livery, devoid of lining, emphasised the utilitarian aspects of the design. In common with the 'Hastings' units, the bogie design proved to be rough-riding, although subsequent modifications had some effect; with provision of hydraulic dampers and other changes to the suspension system.

This first batch of 18 two-car sets was built before the 'Hastings' buffet car sets, and were numbered Nos 1101-1118. Four more followed, Nos 1119-1122 for service in East Sussex. All these had 500hp engines when new. Problems of overcrowding were experienced and it was decided to build the next batch of 'Hampshires' (as they became known) as

three-car sets. To cater for the extra trailer, the engines fitted had their horsepower increased to 600, using a larger Napier turbocharger. In due course the original 18 'Hampshires' also received an additional trailer each, and they were likewise fitted with 600hp engines. These engines had originally been ordered for the second batch of 13 six-car 'Hastings' sets, and the 26 engines were diverted to 22 'Hampshires' and four East Sussex units, whose original 500hp engines went instead to the 'Hastings' units.

In 1963 'Hampshire' unit No 1129 was experimentally fitted with a Dorman 12QT 12-cylinder engine, rated at 725hp for use in a three-car set, (its designed rating was actually 910hp). As discussed in the Introduction, this was an evaluation of the design at a time when there was a proposal to build new four-car DEMUs for a Brighton-Cardiff service, which never materialised. The Dorman engine proved troublesome in service, although giving passengers a quieter and smoother journey, due to its twelve cylinder layout, and it was soon replaced by the rugged but reliable EE Co 4-cylinder 4SRKT unit. A feature of the EECo engine which counted against it was its weight, and although a 6-cylinder version was available (and would have provided valuable extra power) it was found to be too heavy to be installed in a passenger carriage; thus 600hp from four cylinders was the maximum the SR could obtain.

In 1962 the Reading-Portsmouth services had received seven new 'Hampshire' three-car sets to the same basic design, which marked the end of construction of this type; the rest of the 1962 order being for the more modern 'Oxted' design; these units being discussed in the following section.

During 1979, unit No 1111 underwent an extensive refurbishment at Eastleigh works, and was reclassified as 3H(M) which meant three-car Hampshire modified. It had gangway connections fitted between vehicles within the set; fluorescent lighting; public address system and brighter wall surfaces and furnishings. The first class accommodation was removed and all seating was in second class saloons. Externally it was recognisable (when first introduced) by the change from plain blue to blue and grey livery. This unit was renumbered in 1986 as No 205101, being the only example of Class 205/1. No further sets have been refurbished in this style, and it would now appear that the 'Hampshires' will run out of time without much change. Like their 'Hastings' contemporaries they have given reliable service, but have kept the passenger environment firmly back in the 1950s; in stolid comfort.

Above left:
Blue-liveried '3H' unit No 1127 leaves Netley on a Portsmouth-Salisbury working in July 1968, with the DMBS leading. *John H. Bird*

Left:
No 1127 is seen again, this time approaching Basingstoke with the 11.24 Salisbury-Reading of 3 December 1977. Comparison between the two views demonstrates the difference in the two sides of the driving motor vehicle. *Brian Morrison*

Above:
Nowadays the 'Hampshires' sport full blue and grey BR livery, with yellow ends, and are kept in a very presentable condition by the SR. Unit No 1126 is seen here at Portsmouth Harbour station 20 June 1984, on a Salisbury working. *Colin J. Marsden*

Right:
'Hampshire' set No 1131 is one of the later batch, and can be recognised as such by the much smaller route indicator box on the front end (compared to the depth of the driving cab windows — see previous illustration). The DEMU is pictured at Portcreek Junction on the 16.03 Eastleigh-Portsmouth Harbour train on 12 June 1982. *Colin J. Marsden*

3 Eastleigh Works, BR. Branch Line & Local Services 3-Car. Class 207 (SR Class 3D)

Introduced: 1962
Purpose: Oxted line passenger services, and associated branches.
No of cars per unit: 3
TOPS Class: 207
Engine: English Electric Co 4SRKT
Horsepower: 600
Transmission: Electrical. Two nose-suspended axle-hung traction motors
Body: 64ft×9ft/63ft 6in×9ft*
Unit Nos: 1301-1319
Brake Type: Auto-air/Electro-pneumatic
Maximum speed: 75mph
Coupling restrictions: Within SR diesel-electric MU types only
Original Running Nos/Vehicle type/Weight: S60126-S60144 DMBS, 56 tons. S60600-S60618, TC, 31 tons. S60900-S60918, DTS, 32 tons

This fleet of 19 three-car DEMUs for the Oxted line services can be regarded as the most modern examples in Southern Region service today. Built at Eastleigh in 1962 they had the benefit of some industrial design advice from the BTC Design Panel; although in basic layout they still adhered to the Eastleigh drawing office ideas, which meant that there were no gangway connections between vehicles, and slam doors to every seating bay or compartment. However, the interiors were panelled in attractive Formica shades and the seats had improved upholstery, giving a more cheerful appearance. Externally, the immediately noticeable change was to the front ends; which had a more pleasing outline. The entire end was fabricated in steel-reinforced fibreglass with rounded extremities, and the air pipes and jumper cables were neatly housed in recesses, with a wrap-round grab rail above them.

The 'Oxted' sets were built with 8ft 6in wide bodies due to restricted clearances in the tunnels at Tunbridge Wells, but unlike the flat sides of the even narrower 'Hastings' units, they had a curved body profile, which enhanced their appearance considerably. The EE Co 600hp engine, the generator, the traction motors and associated equipment were all to the same SR standards, but a change was made to the layout of the centre trailer; unique to this type of unit. The first class accommodation, in compartments with side corridor, was placed in the middle of the layout, with a toilet at the end. To each end of the layout, open saloons were provided for second class passengers; one end having two bays, the other end three. Just as in the case of the 'Hastings' and 'Hampshire' units the bogies (although of a modified single bolster design) gave a less than perfect ride at speed; by far the most comfortable passenger area being in the centrally placed first class compartments!

In present day blue and grey livery, the 'Oxteds' betray remarkably little signs of age, and with the East Grinstead line electrification now approved, it will be of some interest to see what the future has in store for the class.

Below:
The 'Oxted' sets — as they became popularly known — had a less restricted body profile than their 'Hastings' cousins and there was a curved body profile — nevertheless they were narrower than the 'Hampshires', due to some restricted clearances on the routes for which they were intended. An effort was made to improve the front end design, at the instigation of the BTC Design Panel, and a moulded glass fibre cab front was introduced, with the jumper cables and sockets recessed in two housings, one below each cab window. A continuous handrail was taken across the middle of the cab front and round to the sides; this handrail was originally painted orange; the livery being standard SR green. Set No 1303 was photographed working a Hastings-Ashford train at Hamstreet & Orleston on 30 June 1962. *Dennis C. Ovenden*

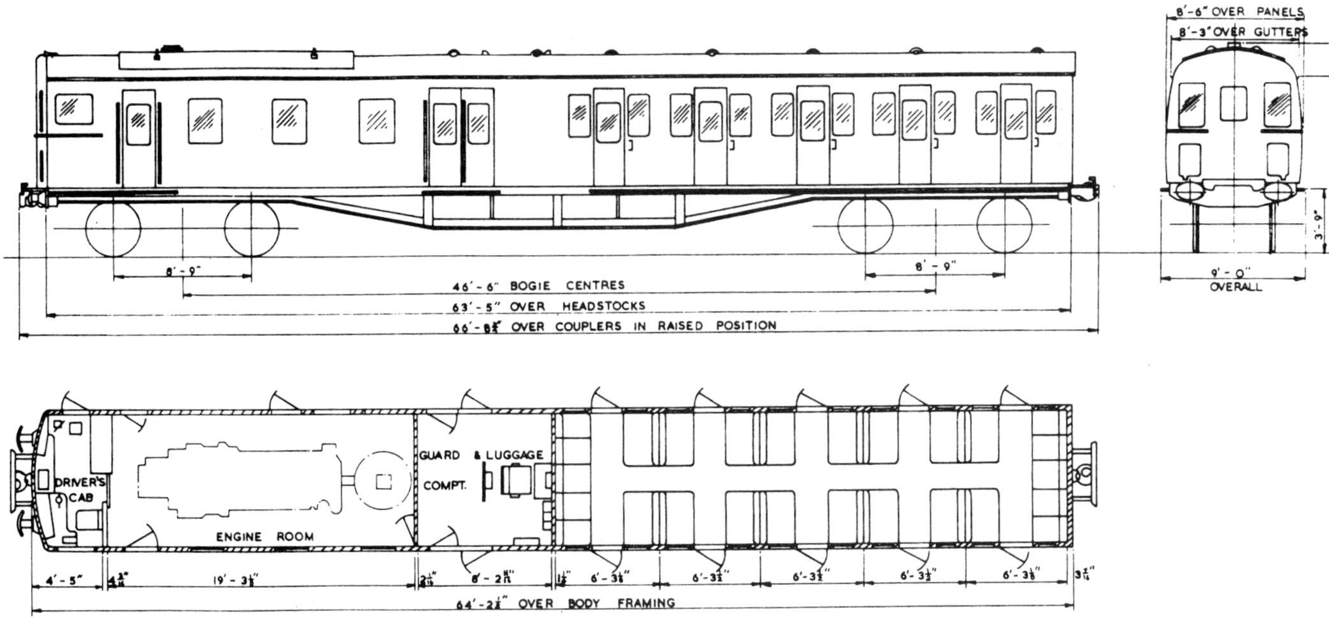
8'-6" OVER PANELS
8'-3" OVER GUTTERS
10'-5" TO GUTTERS
12'-6⅜" OVERALL
3'-9"
9'-0" OVERALL
8'-9"
8'-9"
46'-6" BOGIE CENTRES
63'-5" OVER HEADSTOCKS
66'-8⅜" OVER COUPLERS IN RAISED POSITION
DRIVER'S CAB
ENGINE ROOM
GUARD & LUGGAGE COMPT.
4'-5"
19'-3½"
8'-2⅞"
6'-3⅜"
6'-3½"
6'-3½"
6'-3½"
6'-3⅜"
64'-2½" OVER BODY FRAMING

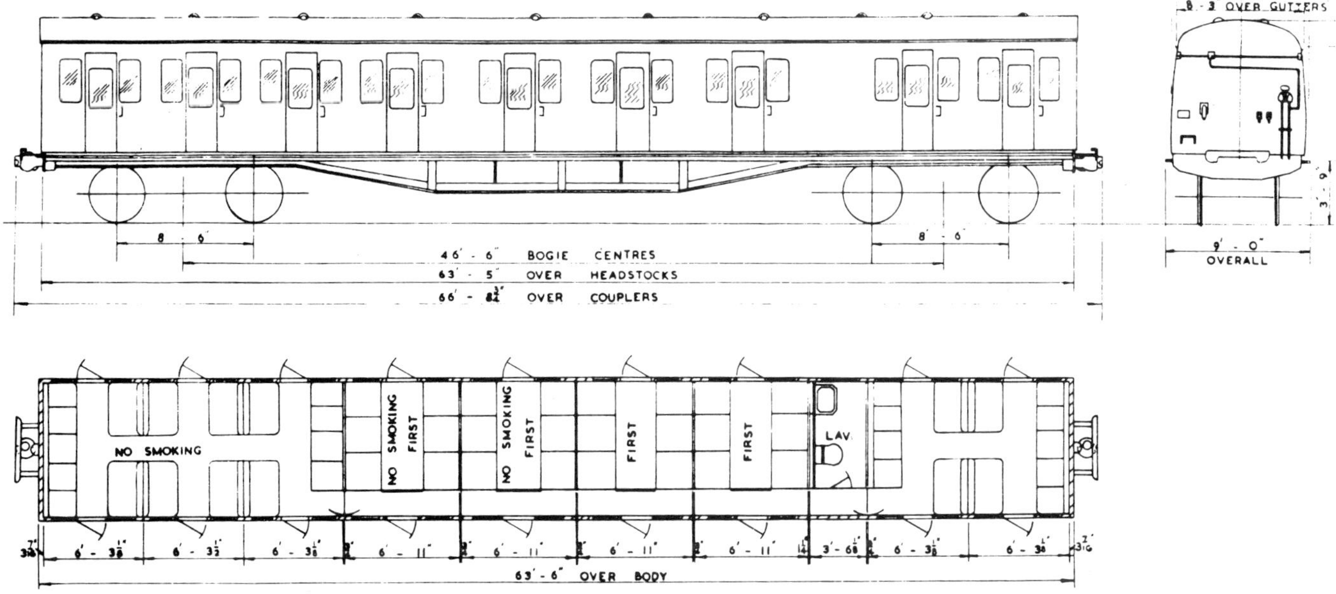
8'-6" OVER PANELS
8'-3 OVER GUTTERS
10' 5" TO GUTTERS
12'-2⅞" TO ROOF
3'-9"
9'-0" OVERALL
8' 6'
8' 6
46' - 6" BOGIE CENTRES
63' - 5" OVER HEADSTOCKS
66' - 8¾" OVER COUPLERS
NO SMOKING
NO SMOKING FIRST
NO SMOKING FIRST
FIRST
FIRST
LAV.
6'-3⅜"
6'-3½"
6'-3⅜"
6'-11"
6'-11"
6'-11"
6'-11"
3'-6⅞"
6'-3⅜"
6'-3⅜"
63'-6" OVER BODY

Top:
The drawing depicts a driving motor brake second (DMBS) of the Class 207, 'East Sussex', or 'Oxted' DEMUs; with restricted loading gauge of 9ft 0in overall. There are no gangways fitted within the set.

Above:
The trailer composite (TC) is illustrated here, with the first class accommodation in compartment-style layout with side corridor access, flanked on each side by small second class saloons. The solitary toilet was only available to travellers in this particular carriage, out of the three in each set, due to the lack of gangway connections. It is difficult to comprehend the reasoning behind such a primitive layout, produced at such a relatively late date in the BR Modernisation Plan. Dr Beeching was a regular traveller on these trains, as he lived near East Grinstead — one wonders if he himself was suitably impressed!

1315
37

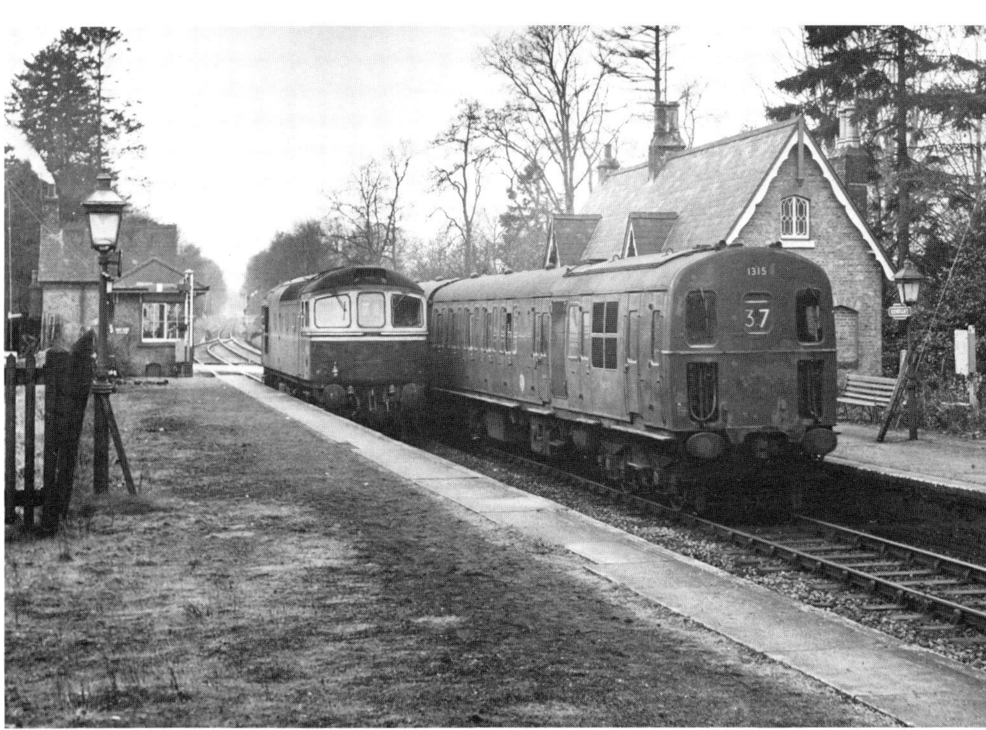

Right:
The 13.08 Three Bridges-East Grinstead service passes a BRCW Sulzer Type 3 Bo-Bo, working light engine, at Rowfant on 22 March 1964. Branch line closures — this one included — made under the Beeching administration made the 'Oxted' sets too numerous for their original duties and led to their use on other SR routes. *G. D. King*

Above:
About to plunge into the tunnel at the northeast end of Brighton, London Road station, this 'Oxted' DEMU was on a through Brighton-London (Victoria) train, via Uckfield and Oxted, on 19 March 1967. The yellow band at cantrail level on the centre trailer clearly denotes the first class accommodation. *John A. M. Vaughan*

Left:
Another tunnel; this time Grove tunnel, just north of Tunbridge Wells, with set No 1313 leaving on the 14.58 service to Tonbridge on 30 May 1981. This view emphasises the front end treatment of this class of DEMUs, with the recessed housings and continuous handrail; also the small headcode box, and two brackets for oil lamps. *R. S. Freeman*

Below left:
In common with the other SR DEMU classes, the 'Oxteds' or Class 207 (3D) East Sussex sets, to give them their official title — are nowadays in BR blue and grey livery, with full yellow warning ends, and have never looked in better shape externally. Set No 1319 is seen on an unusual working for the class, at Reading West on the 12.58 Portsmouth Harbour-Reading duty on 26 June 1982; perhaps running in after a visit to Eastleigh works. The leading carriage is a driving trailer second and thus does not carry the black inverted triangle on the yellow front end.
D. E. Canning

Above right:
Still very active — although the East Grinstead electrification will affect their future to some extent — the 'Oxted' sets are the most modern of the SR DEMUs. Set No 1318 is seen here leaving Tonbridge with the 16.15 to Eridge on 8 April 1982. *Alex Dasi-Sutton*

Right:
Class 207 unit No 1317 leads Class 205 No 1115 on an evening rush-hour London Bridge-Uckfield train leaving Forest Hill on 1 July 1983. *Alex Dasi-Sutton*

4 Eastleigh Works, BR. Cross-country Services 3-Car. Class 206 (SR Class 3R)

Introduced: 1964 (converted)
Purpose: Reading-Guildford-Redhill-Tonbridge route
No of Cars per unit: 3
TOPS Class: 206
Engine: English Electric Co 4SRKT
Horsepower: 600
Transmission: Electrical. Two nose-suspended axle-hung traction motors
Body: 58ft × 9ft*/63ft 11½in × 9ft 3in†
Unit Nos: 1201-1206
Brake Type: Auto-air/Electro-pneumatic
Maximum speed: 75mph
Coupling restrictions: Within SR diesel-electric MU types only
Original Running Nos/Vehicle Type/Weight: S60002-S60007, DMBS*, 54tons 2cwt. S60503-6/9/10, TS(L)*, 29 tons. S77500/3/7-10 DTS†.

Notes: *originally Hastings main line vehicles (see Section 1). †Long underframe, full width Driving Trailer Semi-Compartment Seconds; from 2-EPB electric sets. Some seating space given over to luggage/parcels accommodation. All this class have now been disbanded, and the vehicles reformed into Hastings sets (narrow-bodied vehicles), or Class 204 three-car sets (see Section 5). Set No 1206 ran with long-underframe DMBS No 60037 and TS No 60702 in final period of service.

The late Dr Richard Beeching is on record as having said that he much disliked being called the 'axe man' and of being accused of 'slaughtering' large parts of the BR system. Nevertheless, as the author well recalls, this was precisely the prevailing mood at the time, as each fresh swing of the infamous 'axe' saw yet another portion of line razed to dust and, in most cases, gone forever. Even lines which had recently received new diesel railcars were not immune to the death sentence; whilst those still worked by steam were distinctly suspect at the height of the so-called 'economy cuts'. One such line was the cross-country route between Tonbridge, Redhill and Reading.

Some 20 years later it seems incredible that this direct and strategic cross-country link should have been threatened with extinction. At the time there was a very considerable public outcry, although in reality the service was in poor shape, with outdated rolling stock, and bad timekeeping, with many delays at Redhill and Guildford in particular. No money was available to provide the much-needed new diesel-electric multiple-units which — from recent experience in Hampshire — the SR *knew* could rescue the service, in terms of reliability and economy. Someone at Waterloo then had a very bright idea indeed, and at virtually no expense, six DEMUs were made available in 1964, and indeed saved the day. These DEMUs rejoiced in the unflattering name of 'Tadpoles', due to their odd mixture of two narrow-bodied 'Hastings' vehicles and one distinctly wider normal loading gauge driving trailer.

To create the 'Tadpoles', three of the original short-underframe six-car 'Hastings' units were taken out of service, and the six power cars and some of the trailer seconds were coupled to spare long-underframe 9ft 0in wide driving trailers taken from Class 2-EPB electric multiple-units, to form three-car DEMUs. There was no gangway between the wide-bodied

Below:
Was there ever a more dismal-looking train than the 'Tadpole' DEMU in its original guise? In plain SR green, and with oddly contrasting carriages, it was a combination of pieces put together for a purpose. That purpose was to save the Reading-Redhill-Tonbridge line from closure, and to that effect the 'Tadpoles' succeeded, and we should indeed salute their memory! But if only they had possessed some glamour and comfort, what greater success might have been realised when steam was ousted by diesel on this cross-country route! Unit No 1203 is seen leaving Redhill with the 1.04pm to Tonbridge on 4 June 1965.
J. Scrace

Above:
The nickname of 'Tadpole' was created because of the odd appearance of the two narrow-bodied 'Hastings' vehicles attached to a standard-width driving trailer (which was imagined to be the 'head' of the tadpole, although in reality the tail!). A small yellow warning panel does little to enhance the drab appearance of set No 1204, with the driving trailer nearest the camera — as it heads away on a typical stopping train duty. Note the oil tail lamp still carried. As yet the use of illuminated red blinds in the headcode boxes had not been approved. *Ian Allan Library*

Left:
The change to overall BR blue livery in no way enhanced the beauty of the beast; except that a touch of colour was perhaps provided by the overall yellow warning ends. Set No 1205 is seen approaching Shalford with a Reading-Tonbridge train on 19 May 1978, with the former 'Hastings' driving motor brake second (DMBS) leading. Note that the obligatory inverted black triangle is missing from the front end in this instance. *Colin J. Marsden*

driving trailer and the open second trailer, but the gangway was retained between the two ex-'Hastings' vehicles. Part of the interior layout of the ex-2-EPB driving trailer was cleared of seats to provide additional mailbag/luggage space; a particularly important requirement of this route.

The makeshift 'Tadpoles' performed good service on the whole, often aided by spare 'Hampshires' or 'Oxteds'; traffic was recaptured and the future of the line assured. With the development of Gatwick Airport a stage was subsequently reached whereby the 'Tadpoles' and the other available SR DEMUs were insufficient to provide a new service which the planners envisaged. This service was to link Reading (convenient for London, Heathrow Airport) Redhill and Gatwick Airport, with the Tonbridge services retained. Once agreed, it was on the basis of introducing diesel-mechanical railcars on to the SR; hitherto regarded as distinctly 'foreign' and undesirable! It required a lot of driver-training and changed attitudes before the replacement diesel-mechanical units settled-in (they were mainly Class 119 'Cross-Country' three-cars sets, based at Reading WR depot) and then the valiant 'Tadpoles' were disbanded, during 1979-81, so that by early 1983 only one set remained, and even that had been modified by exchange of vehicles (see below).

Towards the end of their sojourn on the Reading-Tonbridge services a start was made in repainting the 'Tadpoles' in blue and grey livery. This was because, once replaced by diesel-mechanicals, the power cars were to be returned to the Hastings line for further main line use. The driving trailer cars remained in plain blue (except for set 1206) and when disbanded they were sent to the Hampshire area; as described in Section 5. Set No 1206 was the last 'Tadpole' to remain in service and this was reformed with a long-underframe power car and centre trailer from a Hastings set; the centre trailer being a former first class vehicle, demoted to second. All three vehicles received blue and grey livery. This set, which was regarded rather like a 'regional spare' was finally disbanded in the summer of 1983.

Left:
Judging by the clean ballast, a lot of work had just been undertaken on the trackwork at the northern end of Redhill station in June 1975, when this picture of 'Tadpole' No 1204 was taken; entering the platforms from the sidings as empty stock, to form the 17.09 Redhill-Reading service. The angle of the camera has emphasised the differing widths of the two types of vehicle which were amalgamated to create these somewhat makeshift DEMUs. The set is in plain blue livery. *Brian Morrison*

Bottom left:
Once the replacement of the 'Tadpole' by Western Region diesel-mechanical 'cross-country' Gloucester sets got under way, the former 'Hastings' vehicles were once again summoned unto the main line flock, and received an overhaul and main line blue and grey livery in anticipation. The driving trailers were not required; hence this odd appearance of set No 1203 at St Leonards diesel depot on 30 September 1979, with only the two 'Hastings' vehicles in blue and grey; the driving trailer remaining in blue.
Colin J. Marsden

Right:
'Tadpole' set No 1206 remained in service for sometime after the rest had been disbanded, and seems to have been used as a regional 'spare'; running where needed. It was reformed with a long underframe power car and centre trailer (the latter a former first class side corridor compartment vehicle) and painted in blue and grey livery. Set No 1206 is seen here at Ham Street on the 15.47 Hastings-Ashford train on 27 July 1982. Note the absence of the inverted black triangle.
Colin J. Marsden

Above:
The driving trailer end of set No 1206 is nearest the camera as the last surviving 'Tadpole' enters Appledore station on an Ashford-Hastings duty on the same day as the previous picture was taken. The 'Tadpoles' became extinct when this set was disbanded in the summer of 1983. *Colin J. Marsden*

5 Eastleigh Works, BR. Cross-country and Local Services 3-Car. Class 204

Introduced: 1979 (converted)
Purpose: Hampshire-Wiltshire-Berkshire area services
No of Cars per unit: 3
TOPS Class: 204
Engine: English Electric Co 4SRKT
Horsepower: 600
Transmission: Electrical. Two nose-suspended axle-hung traction motors
Body: 64ft × 9ft 3in/63ft 6in × 9ft 3in*
Unit Nos: 1401-1404
Brake Type: Auto-air/Electro-pneumatic
Maximum speed: 75mph
Coupling restrictions: Within SR diesel-electric MU types only

Original Running Nos/Vehicle Type/ Weight: S60107/60121/60102/3, DMBS, 56 tons. S77500/8/7/3, TS, 30 tons*. S60807/21/02/03, DTC(L), 32 tons.

Notes: *Trailer second vehicles are 63ft 6in long. The out-of-sequence numbering shown above corresponds to the actual formation of vehicles per set, from units 1401-1404

Another example of SR ingenuity was the formation of these four three-car DEMUs in 1979 at Eastleigh; all utilising existing vehicles from various DEMU sets, including the disbanded 'Tadpoles' (whose power cars went back to the Hastings line). The former 2-EPB driving trailers from the 'Tadpoles' were inserted into each reformed unit as a *centre* trailer second, which meant that the driving cab was redundant. The cab was rendered inoperative, for safety reasons, and is kept locked. The buffer heads have been removed, and additional jumper cables are carried. Now in blue and grey livery, the former driving end is painted plain blue. In most respects, including power equipment these sets closely resemble the 'Hampshire' units.

Above:
The four Class 204 three-car DEMUs were formed from 1979 onwards by reforming various spare vehicles, including driving trailers from disbanded 'Tadpoles'. To begin with their livery was plain BR blue, as seen in this picture of set No 1404 entering Bursledon on the 12.23 Portsmouth-Southampton working on 12 June 1982. *Colin J. Marsden*

Below:
The drawing depicts a driving trailer second (DTS) used as a trailer second (cab not working) in the middle of the set — formerly a 'Tadpole' vehicle.

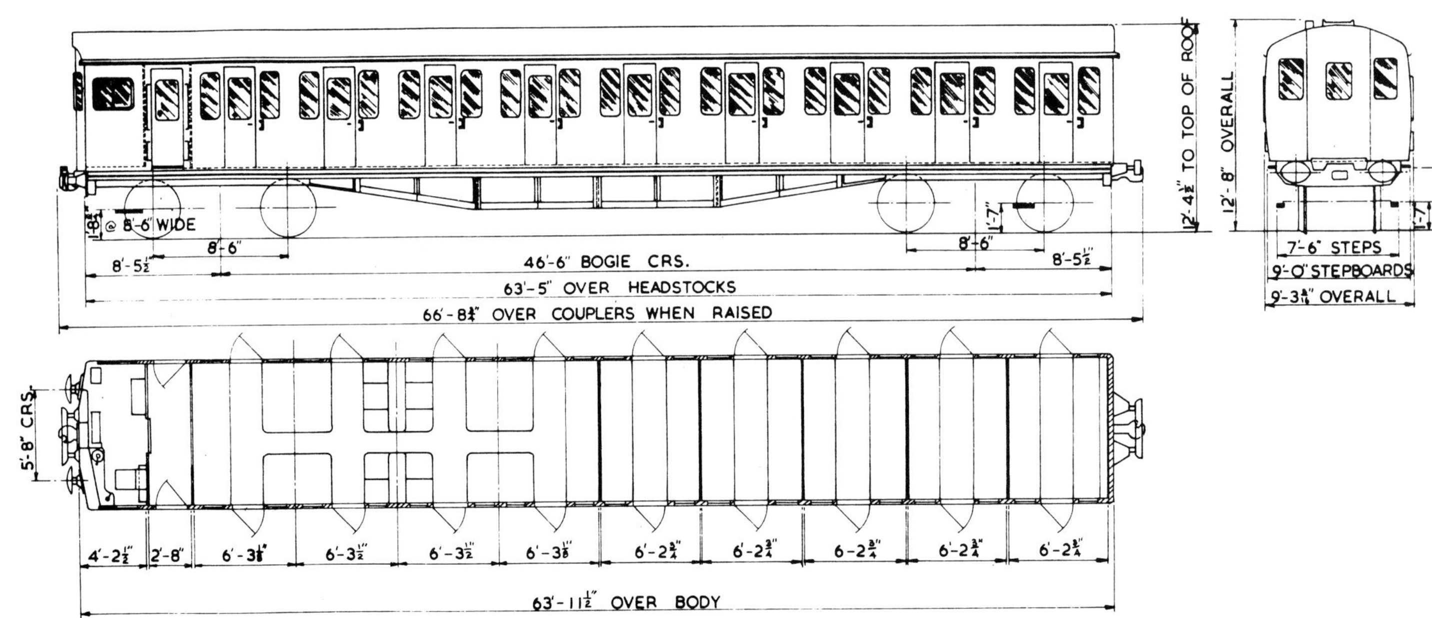

Left:
The redundant driving cab of the centre trailer has been kept *in situ*, locked-up and rendered inoperative. Extra jumper cables are carried on the front, which is painted plain blue. Curiously, the air horns remain on the roof; whereas the side buffers have been removed. Since this interesting detail study was taken, the BR standard blue and grey livery nowadays graces the class, and examples are difficult to distinguish from their 'Hampshire' cousins. *Colin J. Marsden*

Below left:
Class 3T, known also as Class 204, three-car set No 1403 departs from Winchester on a Portsmouth-Reading service. The driving motor brake second (DMBS) is the leading vehicle, and the set carries present-day blue and grey livery. *Colin J. Marsden*

Below:
Class 204 unit No 1402 leaves Whitchurch on 13 January 1986 with the 10.26 Salisbury-Basingstoke. All four members of the class are currently allocated to Eastleigh depot and can usually be seen operating services on non-electrified lines in Hampshire, together with members of Class 205. *D. E. Canning*

Towards the New Generation DMUs: Prototypes, Trials and Tribulations

A feature of the massive investment in British Railways, made possible by the Modernisation Plan of 1955 was that so much new equipment was built at about the same time. Hence, much of it also began to wear out — some 20 or more years later — at the same time; posing an enormous problem of replacement. A particularly severe problem existed with some of the diesel-mechanical multiple-units (DMUs) which were displaying signs of bodywork fatigue, and excessive engine repair/maintenance costs. Even by the commencement of the 1970s it was apparent that a replacement programme would soon be necessary, although in the meantime a compromise programme of refurbishment was also a possibility, to give some breathing space. The SR DEMUs were amongst the most reliable types, although bodywork problems were becoming evident with the 'Hastings' main line sets.

The Modernisation Plan designs of diesel-mechanical railcar, and their subsequent careers are discussed in Part 8 of this series, entitled *Diesel Multiple-Units — The First Generation*; which also covers the refurbishment programme. What we are now concerned with is the dilemma which faced BR's engineers and planners, in searching for more reliable replacement designs for future building. The existing

Top right:
Prototype Class 210 DEMU No 210002 is seen here at Four Oaks station during trials, on 23 September 1982. This was the proposed replacement design for the ageing fleet of first generation diesel multiple-units — typified by the Metro-Cammell set standing on the right. *Chris Morrison*

Centre right:
The 'Alternative Technology' experiment in its first phase, at the Derby Research Centre; simply a bus body, made in modular sections and mounted upon a four-axle rail underframe, and — as yet — unpowered. *British Rail*

Right:
RDB975874 — better known as LEV1 — the lightweight experimental vehicle built as a joint venture between British Rail Research at Derby and British Leyland; with a modular Leyland National bus body section and two bus driving cabs mounted upon a BR-built two-axle underframe. At first it ran trials loco-hauled at speeds up to 80mph to evaluate its riding qualities, then a diesel engine and mechanical transmission were fitted to enable self-powered trials, including passenger service between Ipswich and Lowestoft; as seen here. *British Rail*

fleet (by the year 1980 reduced to around 3,000 vehicles) dealt with a wide variety of duties, although it was on cross-country and secondary services that they excelled, and it was generally considered that they were least successful when used for high-density suburban services, such as operated out of St Pancras, Paddington and in Birmingham. Electrification was seen to be the best solution, if funds became available, for these surburban commuter services, when the DMUs had to be replaced. Because it was unlikely that such wholesale electrification would be authorised in time, it was perceived that a diesel equivalent of an electric multiple-unit, capable of multiple-unit coupling with EMU stock and of running at the same line speeds, would be necessary.

This concept, clearly with the commuter services in mind, was the first stage in the search for a suitable DMU replacement design. Because of the power needed if the performance was to match that of an electric train, to which it could be coupled, the engineers thought in terms of diesel-electric rather than diesel-mechanical equipment. Recent and traumatic experience with fires and other problems on the 'classic' DMUs with underfloor engines and transmission (either hydraulic or mechanical) contrasted badly to the comparative lack of problems encountered by the SR with their diesel-electrics; thus the engineers were much in favour of the latter, with a big diesel engine mounted *above* the underframe and housed in a proper engine room. (One problem with underfloor bus-type engines was their constant exposure to dirt and the elements.)

The English Electric 4SRKT engine was unfortunately no longer manufactured, and it would in any case have posed problems with weight, and overall dimensions (for reasons explained below) although it would probably have been able to provide some 1,000hp installed, due to development work by EE Co on the larger engines in the series. The overall dimensions were limited by the operating people's desire to have through gangway connections between sets, which meant a public passageway had to pass down one side of the engine room — a feature the SR had not required, even in the Hastings main line sets. The final specification called for a four-car set with 1,200hp installed. To obtain the necessary compact layout meant using a highly-rated diesel engine and two quite suitable designs existed — as explained in Section 6. The bodywork was to be based upon the recently introduced integral steel main line Mk 3 carriage and was to be as similar as possible to the new generation of BR standard EMUs (the first being the Class 317 stock for the St Pancras-Bedford electrification) with the same levels of passenger amenity.

At the time, the role of the Class 210 DEMU, as it became known, was to be played in two main areas: **A** commuter services, and **B** non-electrified lines such as in the West Midlands where heavy peak loadings arose. In the case of **A** it was envisaged that the Class 210 was to be the precursor of electrification, and that once the routes chosen were electrified they would be cascaded to other routes *or* disbanded, and their trailer cars used within the new electric trains which would closely resemble them. On certain routes, combinations of EMU/DEMU were thought possible, with the DEMU being uncoupled at the end of the electrified section, and worked forward under its own power to further destinations. Accordingly two prototype sets were authorised and these were to be fully evaluated before production commenced.

Two areas of use for which the Class 210 did not really cater, were the provincial cross-country and secondary services which many of the classic diesel-mechanicals worked; for many of these they were clearly over-specified in terms of construction costs and installed power. Vehicles of lighter weight and more modest power were clearly more at home on such services, although at the commencement of the prototype Class 210 development, BR strongly denied that this 'gap' existed in their future DMU fleet requirements. By the year 1978 it was being widely hinted by some interested parties that the Class 210 was going to price itself out of the market, because the development costs had soared, and by 1981 (when the first prototype was completed) the price of a four car set was put at a staggering £1 million! Some of the Passenger Transport Executives (PTEs) began to question such an expensive replacement diesel multiple-unit, and suggestions began to circulate that BR would be forced to provide an alternative and considerably less expensive railcar design for those who could not afford the up-market Class 210 option in fleet form. Any idea of simply replacing the existing railcars on a like-for-like basis was simply not on because of the changed situation in the railway and road vehicle engine manufacturing industries since 1955; quite a lot of firms having gone out of business altogether, whilst others had ceased manufacture of rail equipment of the kind needed.

Coincidental to prototype development work on the Class 210 DEMU design at Derby, the Research Department there began some tentative investigations into rail carriage body design, know at the time as the 'alternative technology' project, and later on as LEV (Leyland Experimental Vehicle). This began in conditions of some secrecy, and was based upon the idea of using a bus body mounted upon a railway underframe; with the interior laid out in bus fashion. The Leyland National bus, used by many operators, had a body built upon a modular basis, mass-produced in a Workington factory. The comparative cost of this type of vehicle superstructure and that of a typical railway-designed and built railcar, or carriage body was sufficiently different to point to possible ways of economically building railway vehicles, utilising the Leyland expertise. In addition, a four-wheeled vehicle chassis which could ride safely and quite smoothly at speed was a proven part of Advanced Passenger Train (APT) development work; already undertaken at Derby. A marriage of the two produced LEV1; initially a non-powered short underframe four-wheeled trailer with bus-type driving cabs at each end. This first appeared in public view, in a siding alongside the main line at Derby in June 1978 (when the Advanced Passenger Train — pre-production prototype APT-P was being shown to the press). Until then the far less sensational 'alternative technology' project was unheard of and it quite naturally attracted much attention!

In its initial concept the LEV was good common sense, and once it had been tested by locomotive haulage and had demonstrated its stability at speed; the engineers decided to power the vehicle with an underfloor engine and mechanical transmission, and fit it with brakes for service trials, including passengers, once some

Left:
Painted in a bright yellow livery, LEV1 attracted much interest and even had a spell of trial running in the USA (for which it received the protective wire mesh grilles on the windscreen and the bulbous 'forehead' above). It finally returned to the Research Department, having established the concept as a feasible marriage of the two technologies. *British Rail*

Basic data for BRE-Leyland 'R3' Railbus

Overall length	15,300mm (50ft 2¼in)
Wheelbase	8,700mm (28ft 6½in)
Wheel diameter	800mm (2ft 7½in)
Nominal seating capacity	64
Standing capacity	40
Engine type	6-cylinder Leyland horizontal turbocharged diesel
Engine kw (hp)	Over 150 (200)
Transmission	Diesel-mechanical (automatic)
Unladen weight	19.8 tonnes (19.4 ton)
Nominal maximum speed	120km/h (75mph)

Below:
A second prototype, LEV2 was assembled by D. Wickham & Co of Ware, Herts upon a lengthened underframe. This was finished in white livery with a green stripe and was built to the requirements of the Federal Railroads Administration of the USA. This went into trial service on the Boston & Maine Railroad in 1980, where it is seen in this picture in passenger service. A typical American heavyweight railcar stands alongside; making a striking comparison in styles.
D. Wickham & Co Ltd

initial test runs had been undertaken. LEV1 was sent to the USA and ran extensive trials there which sufficiently impressed the Americans for them to commission LEV2. It then returned to Britain for further evaluation.

LEV2 was a distinct advance upon the first essay, and was constructed by Leyland Vehicles and D. Wickham & Co Ltd, to the requirements of the Federal Railroads Administration of the USA. It went into trial service on the Boston & Maine Railroad in 1980. Meanwhile British Rail Engineering Ltd (BREL) and Leyland decided to proceed with another prototype, because of the favourable reactions gained by LEV1, and decided to exploit the export market with it as a joint product, known as the BRE-Leyland Railbus. This was designed as a single unit, fully bi-directional and self-propelled; which could be adapted to multiple-unit operation if desired. This third prototype was known as 'R3'.

Technical details are shown in the table, to which should be added the fact that it could carry 104 passengers (64 seated and 40 standing) and that the vehicle ends were designed to withstand a compression load of 100 tonnes (98 ton) at coupling height. This last factor is of considerable importance in the development story, because it did not match the BR specifications, which were now emerging in an idea for a two-car version of the Railbus. This was the genesis of the Class 140. In August 1981 Roger Ford wrote an article for *Modern Railways* entitled 'The DMU Dilemma', from which the following is an extract:

'On BR, the original LEV — which progressively metamorphosed from an unpowered and unbraked structural test vehicle to a passenger-carrying prototype — sufficiently impressed the Passenger Department for it to sponsor the construction of a two-car version for service trials. There was a clear requirement for a cheaper and simpler DMU to complement the Class 210. The existing DMU fleet includes about 480 two-car units (960 vehicles) for which the Class 210 would not be an economic replacement. Thus was born the Class 140 lightweight DMU.

'The business specification meant that the double-ended back-to-back adaptation of the Leyland National body, while good enough for the railbus, had to be further modified. The requirements included a seating capacity for 102 in the two cars, the elimination of the step-well in the doorway and the provision of a level floor and the installation of a gangway between the two vehicles. More significant, however, were the loading requirements imposed on the completed vehicle structure. These demanded a capability of withstanding the following minimum end loads without permanent deformation:

- 150 tonnes compressive at the couplers;
- 40 tonnes compressive at the base of the body-end pillars;
- 30 tonnes compressive at waist height on the body-end; and
- 30 tonnes compressive at cantrail height on the body-end.

These are now regarded as standard requirements for all new BR multiple-unit construction following the recommendations embodied in the official report on the accident at Chivers occupation level-crossing in December 1976 (Her Majesty's Stationery Office: ISBN 0 11 550479 6). While the recommendations of the Railway Inspectorate do not have the force of law, they cannot be lightly disregarded. Even on rural railways, the risk of collision with heavy farm machinery on unprotected crossings has to be taken into account. In the case of the Class 140, however, the question as to whether the recommended end-loadings have led to over-engineering is somewhat academic in view of the wider role foreseen for the unit. But this matter could become a live issue if the railbus concept were to be adopted by BR for its lowest level of rural services.

'Meeting the end-loadings at the couplers was simply a question of underframe design. But the body end-loading

requirement meant a major change from the railbus/LEV concept. In the Class 140 these loadings are taken by collision pillars attached to the underframe. This arrangement being incompatible with the standard Leyland bus front end, the decision was taken to adapt the standard driving cab designed for the Class 317 EMU and the Class 210. As the layout had already been agreed by BR and the railway trade unions and was in production its adoption saved both time and money in procuring cab equipment. Behind the cab, however, the body consists of standard Leyland National modules, except for longitudinal strengthening of the roof and the doors. While the three railbuses built earlier incorporate standard bus doors, these are unacceptable to BR because they are draughty, and they cannot be secured shut so that, for example (reflecting the wider range of applications planned for the Class 140), they could not resist the pressure pulse of a passing HST. When the Class 140 was being designed BR was investigating a design of double-leaf swing-plug door in service on Netherlands Railways. This has a simple and extremely robust operating mechanism with the door leaves mounted on vertical pillars which simply rotate to open or close. There is an over-centre locking action which provides the wedge or nipping effect needed to maintain an efficient seal.

Above:
British Rail and British Leyland produced another prototype, known as R3, or No RDB977020, which was unveiled at Derby in 1981. This featured a very striking green and orange livery and was altogether longer and sleeker in style than the rather primitive LEV1. This railbus ran passenger service trials on the Western Region between Bristol and Severn Beach for eight months from October 1981. It was then converted to the Irish gauge of 5ft 3in and exhibited at Dublin; afterwards going into service with Northern Ireland Railways. It was put in traffic on the route between Coleraine and Portrush. It is seen here during initial trials on BR; the NIR repainted it in blue and white. *British Rail*

'Inside a Class 140 unit, the main departure from the railbus design is the use of the new standard BR outer-suburban seating, plus the provision of a remarkably compact toilet with a stainless-steel wc pedestal. On the press run of the new train it was emphasised that the design of the prototype had been based on the philosophy: "Let's not argue about detail; cut the cackle and get the train running". Thus the internal configuration should not be regarded as being definitive — the toilet could be taken out to allow more seating space, for example. The heating system uses a mixture of ancient and modern. The modern is the use of the engine coolant to heat the air in the pressure-ventilation system as on the National bus. The ancient, made necessary by the fact that, with prolonged periods of coasting with the engine idling there is insufficient waste engine-heat to warm the vehicle, is an oil-fired water-heater to boost the heating output. This will also be used to pre-heat the vehicles and will aid engine starting in cold weather.

'The underfloor equipment is simply a 1980 version of that found under a classic DMU. The Leyland TL80 six-cylinder turbo-charged engine is horizontally mounted and produces 218hp at 2,100rev/min. The drive to one axle is taken through a four-speed gearbox, one innovation being the incorporation of the reversing gear in the gearbox rather than in the axle final-drive — an arrangement which has given trouble in DMUs in the past. A double-battery system is provided for extra reliability, with one battery exclusively used for engine starting. The turbocharged engine requires a large-diameter exhaust-pipe which means that one engine in the set exhausts at roof height and the other at low level. A device is also fitted which automatically shuts down the engines after 10min idling when the unit is stationary. This is intended to save fuel and is also said to be an aid to reliability.

'With memories of underfloor fires in DMUs still fresh, the design eliminates, as far as possible, horizontal surfaces on which can accumulate debris which then become soaked in oil; and flammable materials and lagging have been eliminated below the floor. Standard fire-detection and extinguishing equipment is fitted and, as a further precaution, there is a continuous 2mm (0.08in) thick steel sheet underneath the vehicle floor from which access hatches to the underfloor equipment have been eliminated. No loss of accessibility is anticipated on production units.

'The two-axle suspension, designated AXI-Pa, is the same derivation from the High Speed Freight Vehicle (HSFV) series used on LEV and the railbuses. It incorporates a coil spring either side of the axlebox with vertical and lateral control through hydraulic dampers and the Flexicoil springs providing lateral stiffness. The axle is located by the longitudinal traction rod between the axlebox and a bracket on the subframe. The wheel tread brake assembly, with its composition blocks, is mounted on the axlebox because of the large degree of freedom allowed to the wheelset by the suspension. The suspension is said to be capable of an acceptable ride performance at speeds up to 80mph.

'The press run with the prototype Class 140 unit was over the 13½ miles between Leeds and Ilkley and return. On pulling away from Leeds my immediate impression was that the new train felt exactly like a classic DMU and not at all like the railbus. Vibration from the engine and track was particularly noticeable and, as the speed increased, the impact of rail joints became most obtrusive, producing a sharp ringing noise at speed. At high speed, say over 50mph, there was pronounced vibration and some resonance in the passenger saloon. Vibration could also be felt through the floor. The ride is best described as lively with considerable bounce and sway; on the fastest part of the return run, most of which I spent standing in the vestibule, the relative motion between the cars was considerable. There is clearly some scope for tuning the suspension — although the unit had already been tried with three other damper

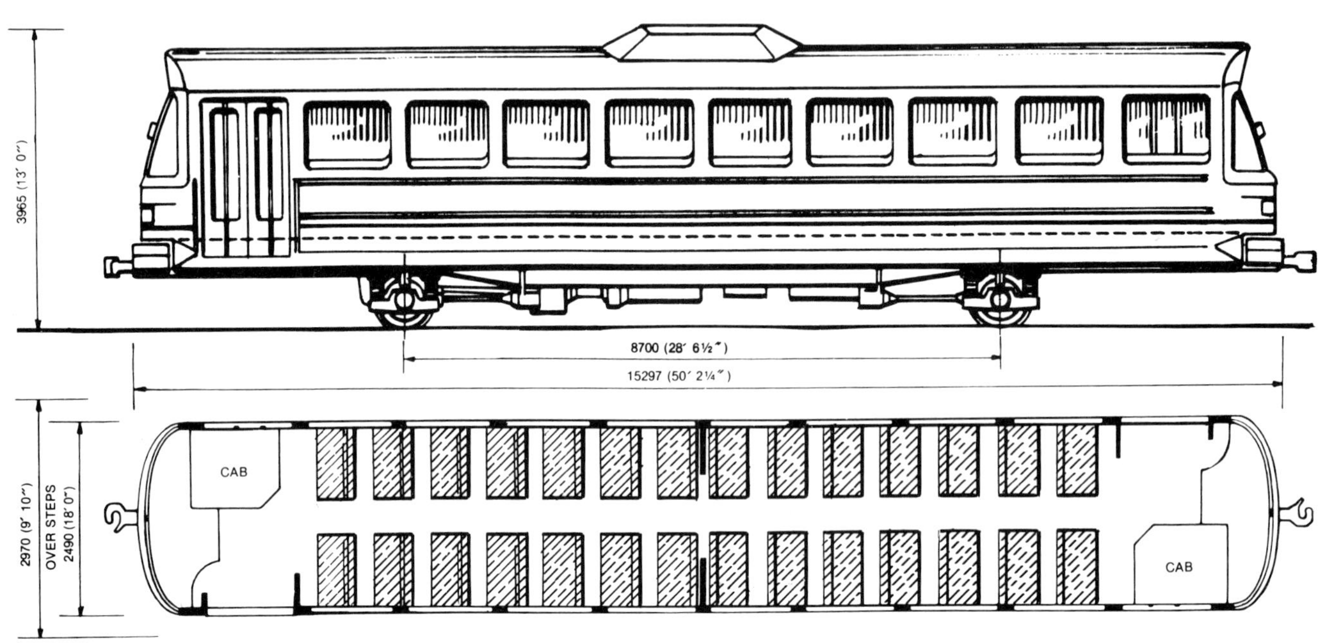

WHEEL DIAMETER 800 (2' 7½") ESTIMATED WEIGHT 19.8T (44000 LB)

The general arrangement of the R3 BRE-Leyland prototype of 1981; later sold to Northern Ireland Railways.

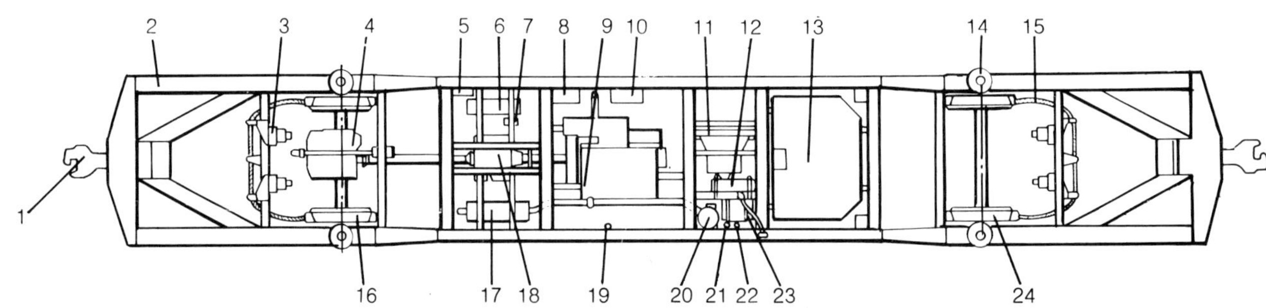

1. Coupler (to suit operators requirements)
2. Underframe structure
3. Brake actuator
4. SCG final drive unit
5. Drive control equipment
6. Auxilliary water heater
7. Water circulating pump
8. Body connection bulkhead
9. Leyland engine
10. Body connection bulkhead
11. Radiator and fan
12. Radiator header tank
13. Fuel tank
14. Body mounting
15. Brake cable
16. Wheelset (powered) and Flexicoil suspension
17. Exhaust silencer
18. SCG gearbox
19. Throttle dip valve
20. Air filter
21. Fuel shut off valve
22. Fuel sedimenter
23. Hydraulic header tank
24. Wheelset (non-powered) and Flexicoil suspension

Above:
The BREL-Leyland 'R3' railbus in Northern Ireland Railways livery at Coleraine on 9 August 1982. *Desmond Crockett*

settings before the current arrangement. In the course of an al fresco conference at Ilkley Mr Keen pointed out that any train rides only as well as the track allows and that "jointed track at 45mph is what the Class 140 likes least".

'The Ilkley press conference also cast more light on BR's policy towards the DMU replacement problem. Referring to a recent article in the *Sunday Times*, Mr Keen denied that the Class 140 was a "glamorous idea from Research (the railbus) taken over by fuddy-duddies and made more like a traditional train". In the Class 140 BR was not looking at a train just for rural branch lines, but also for heavier-duty work such as PTE services. He emphasised that the unit being demonstrated was a prototype and there were many options for changes in production versions, including the doors and front end. There might even be scope for both a cut-price rural version and a more-expensive heavy-duty version. From this it seems that the Class 140 could be developed to fill completely the gap between the refurbished DMUs and the Class 210 and that the upper limit of its capabilities may be raised. On the other hand, my subjective impression is that the 1981 DMU replacement is not so passenger-friendly as the vehicle it is supposed to replace and that the better designs of classic refurbished DMU would be better employed filling the gap between the Class 140 and the Class 210. Much depends on price. Mr Keen was anxious to refute reports that the Class 140 would cost £400,000 and said that the true cost was about £280,000 per two-car set. Apart from the fact that the higher figure was given to the press by BREL at the roll-out of the railbus, it is hard to see how a two-car train with special ends and additional strengthening, heavy-duty doors and non-standard seating and heating can be built for the same cost per vehicle as the railbus with its standard Leyland body.

'BR now has so many options for the DMU replacement problem — from railbus to Class 210 — that it is easy to lose sight of the fact that the need is to replace a single type of vehicle which can do most passenger jobs outside Inter-City adequately rather than one job particularly well. The problem is that tying down the requirements the DMU replacements are supposed to meet is like trying to nail a jelly to a tree. At the top end of the market the need may disappear almost overnight if a big/fast electrification programme is authorised. At the bottom end of the other Provincial Services the popular image of the rural branch line rarely holds water, with seasonal loadings considerably exceeding the capacity of a single railbus. But if the railbus concept is to be moved up-market to become a true multiple-unit the re-engineering involved (and those end-loadings for the Class 140 are essential the moment it moves on to the main line even if they are arguably a luxury out in the country) puts up the cost while producing a modern vehicle which is inferior in ride and noise levels to the classic DMU.

Surprisingly, in all the talk of DMU replacements and railbuses no one seems to have considered the possibility of building a new generation of classic DMUs using the same power train as the Class 140 (now that underfloor equipment is apparently acceptable again) combined with the latest construction techniques and a modern simple bogie. Such a train might not be as cheap as the Leyland-bodied vehicles but neither would it be nearly as expensive as the all-singing all-dancing Class 210. It is surely not without significance that this is precisely the option most favoured by other European railways — most notably by the German Federal, which has more experience than most of the railbuses. While many of the names on the manufacturers' plates on the present BR DMU fleet are no longer in the railway business, Derby and Swindon Works of BREL and Metro-Cammell are still active and hungry for new business. While the prototypes are being evaluated it might be worth BR's while looking at yet another option. *Perhaps the only DMU replacement is another DMU*.'

(The italics for the last sentence are mine.)

I have included this lengthy quotation because it so admirably highlights the problems that were being built into what, originally had been a simple idea. Roger Ford must be commended for his foresight, in view of what has since transpired.

Meanwhile the BREL — Leyland 'R3' single unit, after some trial running on BR, was re-gauged to 5ft 3in and sold to the Northern Ireland Railways, who put it to service on the Coleraine-Portrush branch in August 1982. No further thought was given to the idea of using single units on BR (see below), but the idea of a two-car set persisted, and the search was soon on for an improved version of the Class 140, using more of the original R3 conception, hence this report in the January 1982 issue of *Modern Railways*:

'For "Class 140" read "R4"

The latest development in British Rail's long-running attempt to produce a replacement diesel multiple-unit was leaked at a transport seminar held in London in November. The proposal now is to produce a two-car train combining the "best features" of the BRE-Leyland railbus and the Class 140 lightweight DMU. There is some irony in the fact that the Class 140 itself represented an attempt by BR's Mechanical & Electrical Engineering Department to make the railbus suitable for BR use. This included provision for multiple-unit control and additional heating plus the fitting of an adaptation of the driver's cab module produced for the Class 210 diesel-electric unit, new swing-plug doors (as used on Netherlands Railways), and standard BR inner-suburban-type seating. At a demonstration of the Class 140 in June 1981, notwithstanding these variations from the original bus-on-rail-chassis concept, BR's Chief Passenger Manager Peter Keen was adamant that the two-car unit cost no more than twice the price that had been quoted earlier for the basic railbus — £140,000. It appears that the new unit, code-numbered "R4", is a step nearer the original railbus concept — although the price quoted, £300,000, is some 7% higher than that then given for the Class 140. Salient features of R4 are seating for 100 passengers, a gangway between the two vehicles, a toilet and luggage space. The Class 210-type driver's cab seems to have been abandoned. A single double-ended vehicle has been ruled out on the grounds that only six BR routes have appropriate traffic levels. BR now hopes to build 20 R4 units if the necessary financial support is forthcoming from the Passenger Transport Authorities within whose areas they would operate.'

Above:
By 1982 some doubts were being expressed in certain quarters as to the suitability of either the proposed fleet of Class 210 DEMUs or of Class 140 railbuses as replacements for existing time-worn diesel mechanical multiple-units. The Class 210 was considered too expensive, whilst the Class 140 was considered too small in passenger-carrying capacity. In response to an inquiry by the West Midlands Passenger Transport Executive (WMPTE) the Birmingham firm of Metro-Cammell put forward proposals for a modern diesel-mechanical design — the genesis of today's Class 151 (see page 59). This was the initial artists's impression of what a modern version of the 'classic' DMU might look like. *Metro-Cammell*

Clearly, the Class 140 had been 'over-engineered' in the quest for safety. The Class 141 design was then drawn-up (originally called R4) as a result, and 20 units were indeed authorised, as hoped for. However, at the same time, at the initiative of the West Midlands Passenger Transport Executive (WMPTE) a proposal for a new version of the underfloor-engined 'classic' diesel multiple-unit was being drawn-up by Metro-Cammell Ltd in Birmingham! But this idea had to 'wait in the wings' because BR now wanted to evaluate its own two contenders for what I have chosen to call the 'New Generation DMUs'. These were the Class 210 DEMU and the Class 141 two-car railbus.

Below:
By 1983 British Rail were also having some second thoughts about the future, and about their Class 140 prototype. This was an artist's impression for the Class 141, in which more of the original railbus ideas were once again to feature. *British Rail*

Spotlight on the Class 140: A Solitary Prototype

Above:
The one-off Class 140 prototype two-car unit approaches Par with a crew training run on 18 April 1985. *Steve Turner*

Left:
As related in the text, BR imposed a lot of changes upon the initial concept, in an attempt to match it to standards laid down for rail vehicles over the years. The Leyland National bus-type cab fronts were abandoned and an ugly affair substituted complete with centre door. Despite the description 'lightweight' issued to the press when the prototype Class 140 appeared in 1981, it was anything but that when compared to the original prototypes LEV1 and R3! Here one of the two carriages is seen in an advanced stage of construction. *British Rail*

140001

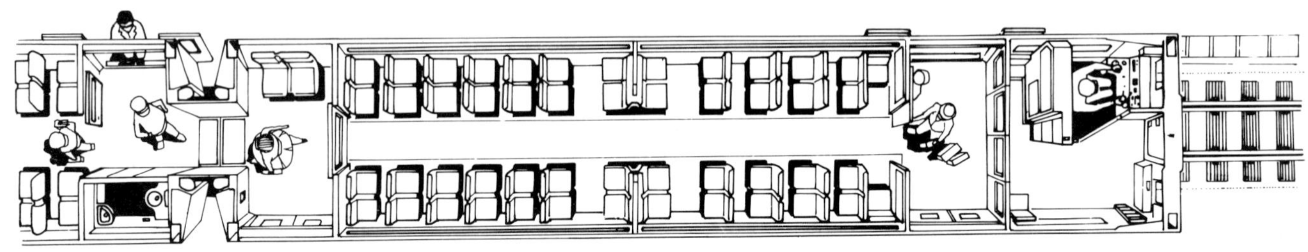

Top left:
Detailed view of the front end of No 140001, showing the poor layout; a visual disaster!
British Rail

Top centre:
Detail view of Class 140 suspension.
Ian Allan Library

Above left:
Interior layout of the Class 140 'lightweight' diesel unit. The seats were of the same pattern as those for the Class 317 EMUs — quite different to the simple bus type seats of the previous prototypes.
British Rail/David Gibbons

Left:
The prototype Class 140 two-car railbus. No 140001 seen at Cattal, on the Harrogate-York branch during a trial run on 29 June 1983. The livery is blue and grey with yellow ends. Note the roof-mounted air horns and MU jumper cables below cab windows.
British Rail

Above:
The solitary Class 140 two-car prototype has been very extensively tested on BR routes, and obviously a great many valuable lessons have been learned. Here the set is seen standing in Platform 4 of Plymouth North Road station on 3 July 1981, having just completed trials on the Bere Alston and Gunnislake branch line. *M. P. Turvey*

Right:
The Class 140 railbus, carrying its class designation above the end gangway, passes westwards through Liskeard station on 19 July 1984. *Brian Cultell*

6 Derby Works, BR. General Purpose Prototypes 3/4-Car. Class 210

Introduced: 1982
Purpose: Prototype units for evaluation on a range of secondary passenger services; from commuter to cross-country
No of Cars per unit: 3*/4
TOPS Class: 210
Engines: MTU 12V396 TC11*/Paxman 6RP200L
Horsepower: 1,140*/1,125
Transmission: Electrical. Four axle-hung traction motors
Body: 65ft 0½in×9ft 3in
Unit Nos: 210001 — 210002*
Brake Type: Electro-pneumatic/Westcode
Maximum speed: 90mph
Coupling restrictions: Only within type and with 1972 type high-density EMU stock (Not SR Class 455)
Original Running Nos/Vehicle Type/ Weight:
60200*, DMS, 63.0 tonnes. 60201, DMBS, 64.5 tonnes.
60400*/1, TS, 26.8 tonnes. 60450, TC, 28.0 tonnes. 60300/1*, DTS, 28.9 tonnes.

Notes: *indicates vehicles forming unit No 210002, which is a three-car set, with GEC electrical equipment; whereas unit No 210001 is a four-car set with Brush electrical equipment.

Looking much more like a modern BR EMU, than a conventional diesel multiple-unit, the prototype Class 210 DEMU made its debut for the press on 20 May 1982. This was set No 210001, with a four-car layout; whereas set No 210002 was a three-car, and had a different engine installed for comparison. The journal *Modern Railways* reported in July 1982 some initial impressions:

'Impressions of the Class 210
To judge by the press trip, the riding of the new diesel units is generally excellent, with a commendably high level of insulation from outside sounds for non air-conditioned stock (although, in truth, the superbly aligned Western Region exit from London scarcely represents the most testing challenge). However, travel in the power car is noticeably more lively and the hum of the diesel engine is clearly audible in the passenger saloon — though not unduly obtrusive.

'While the interior provides a generally bright and airy environment, the non window-related seat layout gives many passengers an extremely poor view outside, made worse by comparison with earlier open-plan sliding-door stock by reason of the high seat backs. Although that may be of little account on commuter lines, where few passengers spend their time gazing at the passing scene, the same cannot be said for some of the longer "tourist" routes on which production units might eventually be expected to operate. The saloon-end view of the line ahead that is one of the more popular features of existing DMU designs is entirely lacking. Moreover, the small-sized windows in the doors of the Class 210 take little account of the natural sight-line of passengers standing in the vestibule, who — unless of

Below:
Class 210 DEMU No 210001, the first of two prototypes, one a four-car (seen here) and one a three-car layout; which BR envisaged as the possible successor to much of the existing fleet of some 3,000 (1982 figures) diesel mechanical/diesel electric multiple-units — most of them by then well over 20-years old. Above-floor diesel engines were installed, and the general design of these Class 210s followed contemporary thinking for the new generation of electric units — today's Classes 317 etc — with which it was designed to be capable of running in multiple. No 210001 is seen at Derby when new. Livery is blue and grey. *British Rail*

less-than-average height — have to stoop to ascertain their whereabouts.

'Both first- and second-class seating is comfortable enough for relatively short journeys — certainly far better than the European norm for vehicles in this category — although the second-class seat frames are somewhat utilitarian in appearance. Internal doors are a mixture of types: conventionally hinged, at the vehicle ends; manual sliding, at the outer ends of the first-class saloon; and two-way flap, separating smoking and non-smoking sections in first class — presenting something of an obstacle course for someone walking through the train, to visit the toilet, for example. That, incidentally, is quite a trek from the far end of the driving trailer. An understandable desire to avoid a proliferation of vehicle types means that both toilets in the four-car units are situated in the composite vehicle. An indication that there are toilets — and in which direction they are located — would surely be helpful.

'The toilet compartments themselves are somewhat oddly arranged, with the mirror located alongside the wc pan, on the opposite wall to the wash basin. Another curiosity is the provision of illuminated signs to inform would-be users when a toilet is "out of order", but nothing to tell them when it is merely "occupied" — apart from the conventional door-lock indicator.

'In overall appearance, the new units are spoilt by some clumsy detailing, evidenced by the angular slit-like hopper-type opening windows, which look like an afterthought set above the main Mk 3-type double glazed units, and by the somewhat untidy arrangement of bodyside ventilation grilles on the power car. But worst of all is the treatment of the units ends, which it is difficult to believe were consciously "designed" at all. Admittedly severe constraints were imposed by the demand for an end gangway — but that requirement can scarcely excuse a singularly characterless "face", with its curious widow's peak (originally intended to house the now redundant four-character headcode indicator?).'

Clearly, there were still some areas for improvement; nevertheless the Class 210 represented an immense leap forward from 1950s standards of design. It was a distinctly "up-market" design with a basic body shell closely based upon the highly successful BR Mk 3 InterCity all-steel carriage, but using pressure ventilation instead of full air-conditioning, and it was fitted with power-operated double sliding doors. An operating requirement was the use of gangway connections for the front ends, enabling passengers to walk from one unit to another, when more than one set formed the train. This meant provision of a corridor down one side of the engine compartment; the engine itself being offset from the centre line of the power car in order to create sufficient space.

As discussed on page 33, the choice of a diesel-electric power unit, mounted above underframe level (in fact, strictly speaking, there is no separate underframe on the Class 210 as the body is an integral structure) was the result of operational experience with BR's existing fleet of different types of diesel unit which had pointed clearly to the advantages of a single high-powered diesel engine, mounted within the car body and coupled to bogie-mounted traction motors, over medium-powered under-floor engines spread throughout the train. The design specification called both for high performance characteristics, closely comparable to those of modern EMUs, and as already mentioned for a through-access facility between units operating in multiple. Taken together, these requirements dictated the use of a compact high-speed diesel engine, mounted off-centre to allow the provision of a side corridor past the engine compartment. Two alternative engines were chosen to power the two prototypes: a German-built MTU 12V-396-TC12 for the three-car unit; and a British-built GEC 6RP200 for the four car. The MTU unit is a 12-cylinder-Vee engine rated at 915kW at 1,500rpm. The GEC power unit is a derivative of the Paxman Valenta (and hence has the advantage of some commonality with the HST power plant); it is a six-cylinder in-line design rated at 839kW at 1,500rpm.

The cooler group is mounted within the engine compartment and so scavenges it of oil mist. The extractor fans are hydrostatically driven from the engine, and there is a positive flow of air from the electrical compartment to the engine compartment.

Each power car carries an underslung tank of 500gal capacity which is sufficient for an operating range of more than 600 miles. In fact, BR engineers claimed an average fuel consumption of 1.7miles/gal, which is rather less than that achieved by the present 'standard' diesel-mechanical units, although the latter cannot match the Class 210's rate of acceleration or 90mph top speed.

Two alternative and interchangeable electric-transmission sets were fitted, from GEC and Brush for the three-car and four-car units respectively. In each case the engine directly drives a main alternator for traction power and an auxiliary alternator for other services. The alternators are housed in a clean-air compartment ventilated by filtered air drawn from outside by the alternator fan. The main alternator is rated at 650A, 1,200V, three-phase ac. Solid-state rectification is provided to handle a continuous current of 1,550A dc. The rectifier diodes are in the clean-air compartment with forced-air cooling.

Each power car has four axle-hung self-ventilated traction motors similar to those fitted to the Class 317 electric stock,

Left:
Interior of the trailer second vehicle of one of the Class 210 prototype units, showing the bright, modern design. Except at doorways, seating is in the 2+3 pattern. *British Rail*

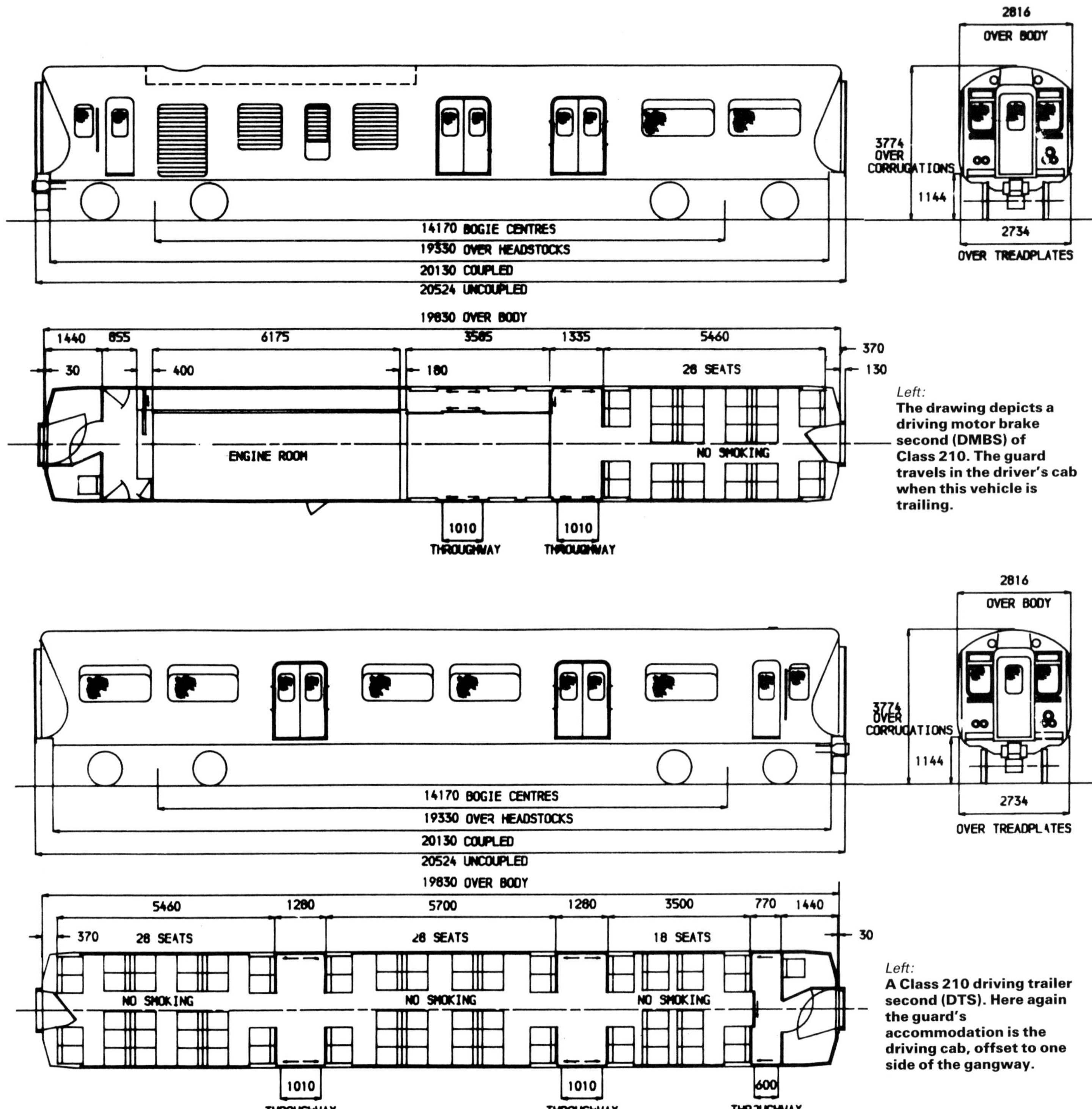

Left:
The drawing depicts a driving motor brake second (DMBS) of Class 210. The guard travels in the driver's cab when this vehicle is trailing.

Left:
A Class 210 driving trailer second (DTS). Here again the guard's accommodation is the driving cab, offset to one side of the gangway.

and each rated at 190kW at 1,630rev/min, taking 335A at 620V.

Tightlock couplers were provided for the outer ends of each unit, with the electrical and air continuity established through automatic connectors mounted below the couplers. Hence there were no fussy jumper cables and receptacles to blemish further what was a rather poorly designed front end. A single electrically driven compressor under the power car supplies air to the braking system, the secondary suspension and the external sliding doors.

The brakes are of the disc type, controlled by the Westcode system which provides three braking steps by de-energising the train wires in a coded sequence. Any interruption of the train circuit, accidental or through operation of the passenger emergency switches, results in a full brake application.

One of the fundamental weaknesses of the first generation BR DMU/DEMU fleet was the poor riding quality provided by virtually every type of bogie that carried them — the sole exception being the type B4/B5 bogie; alas only fitted to a few of the latter-builds. By way of contrast, the Class 210 rides like a dream, even at top speeds of 85-90mph, thanks to much hard work undertaken by the Research people at Derby. The bogie used under the power cars is known as the BP20. Weighing 11.4 tonnes complete and intended for a 19 tonne maximum axle-load, the BP20 design has a wheelbase of 2,710mm (8ft 10¾in). The frame is a box-section structure of welded steel plate fitted with headstocks to carry the brake cylinders which the presence of the traction motors makes it impossible to mount in an inboard position.

The wheelsets have monobloc wheels which carry the brake discs and taper-roller cartridge axle bearings are used. Primary suspension consists of Clouth rubber springs with hydraulic dampers. Secondary suspension is by air springs controlled by means of levelling valves to ensure that the vehicle is maintained at a fixed height under all conditions of load. Vertical damping is by connecting each air spring to an auxiliary reservoir through a choke, while lateral movement is controlled by a

Top:
Set No 210002, with a three-car layout, also differed in having a German-built MTU engine installed for comparative purposes; the first unit had a British-built GEC derivative of a Paxman engine. No 210002 was photographed at Southall Depot (WR) on 4 January 1983, during trials. Note that on this unit the aluminium surrounds to the windows on the front end were left unpainted. *Alec Swain*

Above:
Close-up of a trailer composite (TC) vehicle in a Class 210 set. The resemblance to the Class 317 St Pancras-Bedford EMU design is remarkable, and quite intentional; it being envisaged at one time that the 210s could work in multiple with the electric sets, providing identical passenger accommodation. *Colin J. Marsden*

Below:
Once the bright hope of BR, but too expensive to build in many people's opinion, there may still exist a future role for a limited fleet of Class 210s, on some cross-country routes; but this remains to be seen. Meanwhile the two prototypes continue to amass mileage in BR service as is seen here with set No 210001 running on trials. Note the third vehicle from the camera, which has the limited amount of first class accommodation, located between the two sets of sliding doors, in the centre. *Jeremy de Souza*

single hydraulic damper. Torsion bars are used to control body roll. There is a bogie pivot mounted on the body underframe, but this is relieved, by means of a rubber-bushed linkage, of all but traction and braking forces.

The trailer bogie is of the BT13 type, similar to that which had already been fitted to some 500 existing EMU vehicles. Designed for a 12 tonne maximum axle load, it has a 2,600mm (8ft 6½in) wheelbase and itself weighs 4.7 tonnes. The frame is a lighter version of the BP20 without the headstocks. The secondary suspension is similar to that of the BP20, with secondary air springs, but the primary suspension consists of chevron rubber springs mounted above the axleboxes for which trailing-arm registration is provided.

No one could deny that the Class 210 was a high quality replacement for an ailing fleet of railcars — but, equally no one could deny it was extremely expensive. In 1982 production costs were put at £965,000 for a three-car unit and £1.3 million for four cars. It was too expensive and too sophisticated to suit many needs, and meanwhile a challenge had appeared in the somewhat austere but very much cheaper shape of the Class 140 prototype two-car railbus!

Nonetheless the two Class 210 sets have undertaken — and indeed today are still undertaking — considerable trials in service conditions. There may still emerge a role for a DEMU of such fine capabilities — as a secondary InterCity service unit, for example — although some cost-cutting exercises will be necessary if it is to become viable. Of some interest is the fact that the Northern Ireland Railways (NIR) ordered some three car 'Castle' class DEMUs in 1983/84 which could be described as an evolutionary Class 210. These NIR DEMUs closely follow the design of the Southern Region's Class 455 electric trains in all respects except the provision of a separate underframe and an independent diesel-electric power unit. Perhaps history will repeat itself, and just as BR has never run a Mk 2 DEMU, whereas NIR does, once again BR may never run a *production* Mk 3 DEMU!

Formation of Class 210 units

	Seating capacity	
Three-car unit	*1st-cl*	*2nd-cl*
Driving motor second	—	45
Trailer second	—	84
Driver trailer second	—	74
	—	203
Four-car unit		
Driving motor brake second	—	28
Trailer composite with lavatory	22	46
Trailer second	—	84
Driving trailer second	—	74
	22	232

7 British Leyland/BREL Derby. Local & Secondary Services 2-Car. Class 141

Introduced: 1983
Purpose: Local and secondary services
No of cars per unit: 2
TOPS Class: 141
Engines: Leyland TL11, turbo-charged
Horsepower: 400
Transmission: SCG automatic gearbox and final drive
Body: 30.5m×2.50m
Unit Nos: 141001-141020 (not carried)
Brake type: Air. Twin-pipe
Maximum speed: 75mph
Coupling restrictions: Within units of same class
Original Running Nos/Vehicle Type/ Weight: 55502-55521, DMS, 26 tonnes. 55522-55541, DMS(L) 26.5 tonnes.

The Class 140 prototype two-car railbus — with all the added requirements which had led it away from the initial 'pure' Leyland-bodied lightweight design (LEV 1 etc) — departed in too many respects from the ideas being canvassed by the railbus team of BREL and Leyland who had produced the R3.

To recap briefly, the Class 140 was built as a two-car unit and made significant departures from the single-vehicle R3, incorporating as it did much standard railway equipment. The additions included Class 210-type cab layout, body-strengthening, power doors, standard BR seats, and a toilet. Critics including the journal *Modern Railways*, soon assailed the Class 140 by claiming that the original railbus concept (a rail vehicle that could be cheaply produced by drawing on road vehicle production capacity) had been unacceptably diluted, and that if such a heavily-engineered unit were to be produced it would be better to 'go the whole hog' and produce a replacement DMU by conventional methods in railway workshops. As a result of such criticism, a rethink resulted in the Class 141, which reverted to the R3 concept, and many of the modifications featured in the 140 unit were dropped in the 141 units. The Class 141 retains a toilet and was designed and

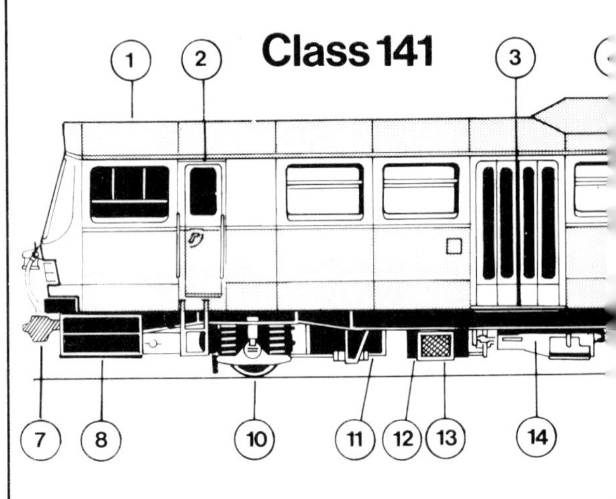

Right:
Layout of the Class 141 two-car set.

Bodyshell
1 Driving compartment, **2** Hinged crew door, **3** Power-operated folding passenger doors, **4** Heating and ventilation 'pod', **5** Exhaust pipe, **6** Corridor connection, **6a** Toilet compartment.

Underframe
7 Tightlock automatic coupler, **8** Start battery, **9** Auxiliary battery, **10** Non-powered axle, **11** Fuel tank, **12** Radiator, **13** Radiator grille, **14** Leyland turbo-charged diesel engine, **15** Automatic gearbox, **16** Powered axle, **17** Traction rod, **18** Exhaust pipe, **19** Air reservoirs and brake equipment, **20** Bar coupling, **21** Engine exhaust silencer, **22** Pre-heater. *David Gibbons*

'Railbus' concept

Leyland 'National' body

Underframe

Radiator

Turbocharged diesel engine

Automatic gearbox

Drive shaft

Final drive

David Gibbons Mar '84

Left:
The basic concept of the two-axle Railbus Class 141 is extremely well explained in this drawing. *David Gibbons*

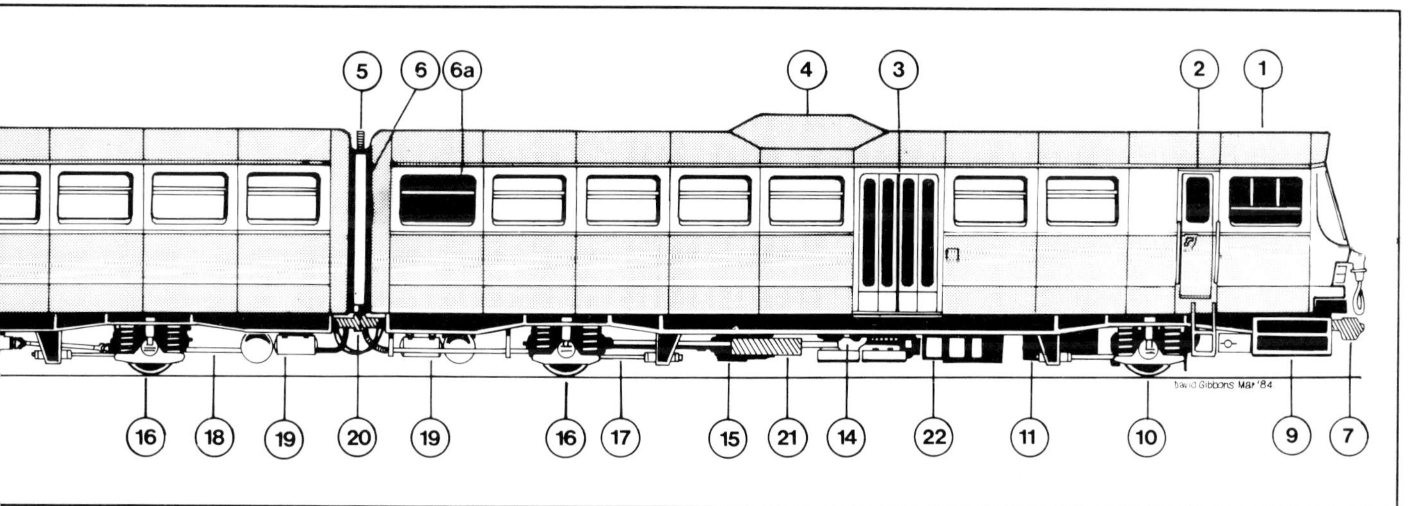

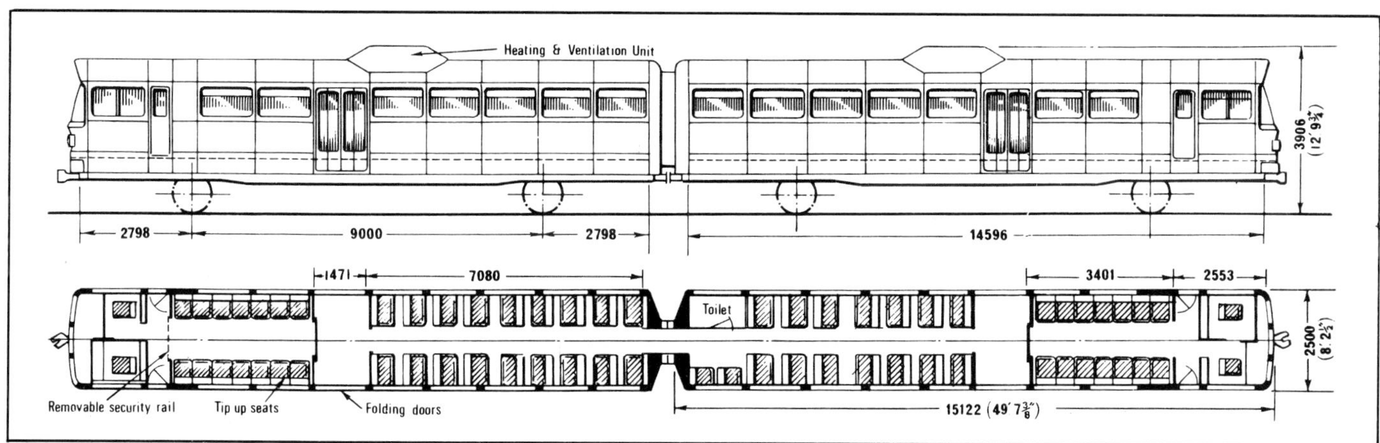

Above:
General dimensions and interior layout of the Class 141 railbus. Note the amount of space taken up by the driving cabs, in proportion to the passenger seating; also the swing doors behind each cab.

Left:
The first production Class 141 two-car DMU railbus, which was demonstrated to the press at Neville Hill, Leeds on 28 September 1983, on what was called 'Urban Transport Day'. It was finished in a slightly non-standard blue and grey livery (the purple-blue being the shade of Barrow Corporation's buses!) with full yellow ends. Considerable refinement was apparent, compared to the Class 140. The front end design in particular was a great advance, but there were still some critics, who complained about the narrow body, cramped 2+2 seating, and the sometimes harsh riding of the two-axle layouts.
West Yorkshire Passenger Transport Executive

produced as a two-car unit, but with a bus-type interior. Also it has been found that the end-loading requirements did not in actual fact require such heavy re-engineering of the National bus body as originally thought. The Department of Transport therefore authorised production of 20 Class 141 two-car units, because it was decided not to build a prototype, due to the amount of experience already gained with LEV1/2 and R3, and the Class 140 prototype. BREL and Leyland also decided to build a further set at their own expense for overseas demonstrations, because by this time many railway administrations were showing some interest in the railbus. This demonstrator went to the Far East and has now run extensive mileages in Thailand, Malaysia and Indonesia.

The Leyland National body is produced in a highly mechanised single-purpose bus-building plant at Workington. The body is made up of modules 1,421mm long, which can be joined to form a vehicle body of any practical length, although the width for road vehicles was fixed at 2,500mm (approximately 8ft 2½in) compared to the normal BR vehicle width of 2,816mm (approximately 9ft 3in). The body modules are built into a chassis, all the sub-assemblies and main assemblies being riveted together using precision jigs. No welding is used in the process. After this, the entire body module for each railbus vehicle is transferred to BREL's Derby Litchurch Lane Works, where it is fitted to the rail underframe. The length of each vehicle is 15,122mm (49ft 7⅜in).

Above:
The Workington-built Leyland National bus-type body is seen being lowered on to its Derby-built railway underframe at the BREL Litchurch Lane workshops in Derby. *British Rail*

Right:
The 'new look' in West Yorkshire was soon emphasised by the decision to paint the Class 141 sets in WYPTE green and white livery, which was certainly eye-catching when kept clean. The first unit to carry the new colour scheme was No 141006, seen at the new station at Saltaire in April 1984. *West Yorkshire PTE*

The high degree of accuracy in assembling the vehicle bodyshell enabled all interior finishing panels, floors, and so on to be supplied to Derby already cut to size. The body finishing panels for instance, were secured by means of moulded nylon clips without the use of tools, and all internal wiring consisted of wiring looms with plug and socket connections. The result is that no skilled trades were employed on the body production line.

The business specification supplied by BR for the bodyshell of the 141 contained the following requirements:

a) A seating capacity for the unit (two cars) of 94.

b) The elimination of the step well in the doorway and the provision of a level floor.

c) The provision of a gangway between the two vehicles.

In addition the structure was required to meet the following minimum end loads without permanent deformation:

150 tonnes compressive at the couplers.

40 tonnes compressive at the base of the body end pillars.

30 tonnes compressive at the waist height of the body end.

30 tonnes compressive at the cantrail height of the body end.

These latter requirements were standard to all current designs of multiple units.

As already mentioned the standard Leyland National bus front end was unable to meet these loads, particularly those above floor level, and therefore had to be suitably reinforced, resulting in quite an attractive style of front end; without the end doors for train crew access and emergency use that ruined the appearance of the Class 140. The rail underframe extends to the ends of the vehicle and is capable of withstanding the statutory 150 tonnes compressive load through the couplers. It is also designed to support all the underfloor equipment, including the diesel engine and gearbox.

The standard Leyland National stepwells are included at the passenger access doors on either side of Bay 5 and the doors themselves are the double folding Deans Type used on the Leyland National 2 bus. Crew access doors are provided either side of the vehicle immediately behind the cab. The design of the cab module is such that the driver's door can be locked back into the bulkhead to provide a full width cab separating the crew from the passengers. The cab door also incorporates a burst-through feature so that the driver can evacuate the cab area in an emergency.

The unit uses a roof-mounted heater similar to that of the Leyland National bus, and fed with waste heat from the engine cooling system. Because the interior volume of the Class 141 is greater than that of the road bus, this system is reinforced by means of convector heaters, also fed with engine cooling water. In rail operation, however, the engine spends a considerable portion of time idling with a correspondingly low heat output and it has been necessary to equip the vehicle with an oil-burning water heater to boost the heat output as required. This arrangement also provides a degree of engine pre-heat and will ease starting problems in cold weather. The driver's cab has its own heater.

The Leyland National standard of trim and finish is used, the passenger seats having moquette covers and a modified squab and cushion fixing to ease removal for cleaning and repair. Each twin-car unit has a toilet compartment which is readily accessible to all passengers in the unit. This compartment includes a toilet, wash basin, vanity unit and mirror etc.

There is an underfloor mounted engine provided on both vehicles of the unit. They are Leyland TL 11 six-cylinder horizontal units, turbo-charged to produce 200hp at 1,950rpm. The drive to one axle of the vehicles is taken via the specially-developed four-speed gearbox (see illustration). This gearbox incorporates the free-wheel and reversing gear and promises to give greater reliability than is experienced with the axle-mounted reversing gear on existing diesel multiple-units. Control of engine and gearbox is by means of conventional relays and electro-pneumatic valves. Another aid to improved reliability is the provision of a double battery system on each car where one battery is concerned solely with engine starting; the system is designed to ensure that the engine starter battery is charged preferentially. The batteries are charged by two alternators shaft driven from the engine which have a total output of 120amps at 30V, of which approximately half is available at engine idling speed. A further aid to reliability is a device to shut down the engine after 10 minutes idling with the vehicle stationary. In the event of engine shutdown, a reduced lighting level is automatically maintained for two hours, after which the system switches to emergency lighting only.

Careful thought was given during the design stages, to fire precautions. Underfloor fires have been a problem with the first generation of 'classic' DMUs for many years. So far as possible, horizontal surfaces which can accumulate debris which can become soaked in oil have been eliminated, and no inflammable materials or lagging are used below the floor. The standard Graviner type of fire detection and extinguishing equipment is provided. There is a continuous steel panel 2mm thick underneath the vehicle floor, and trapdoors for access to underframe equipment from inside the vehicle have been eliminated. All materials used inside the vehicles are to BR requirements concerning inflammability; for example all finish-

Above:
Although an improvement on the Class 140 prototype unit, the members of Class 141 could hardly be described as beautiful. No 141015 (unit number not carried) formed of vehicles Nos 55516 and 55536 stands at Wakefield Kirkgate on 7 March 1985. *A. O. Wynn*

ing panels meet the requirements of BS476 Part 7 Class 1 so far as surface spread of flame is concerned.

The two-axle suspension is derived from the design developed for the high speed freight vehicle and the Advanced Passenger Train (APT-E) in its earliest form, and is capable of an acceptable ride performance at speeds of up to 80mph. The axlebox is a yoke shaped casting providing seats for the coil springs on either side of the axle; the upper ends of these springs engage with retaining spigots on the subframe. Vertical and lateral control is by means of hydraulic dampers mounted between the axlebox and the subframe, with the coil springs contributing the necessary degree of lateral stiffness. The wheelset is controlled longitudinally by means of traction rods between the axlebox and a substantial bracket mounted off the sub-frame, the required stiffness being obtained from an assembly of rubber springs at the attachment of the bracket.

The brake assembly is also mounted on the axlebox because the high degree of lateral freedom of the suspension would otherwise make correct alignment between block and wheel tread impossible. The diaphragm-operated brake cylinders operate through a slack adjuster unit and via a brake cable and brake arms to apply cast iron brake blocks to the wheel tread. A spring actuated parking brake is incorpo-

Below:
The narrow body of the Class 141 design cannot go unnoticed when seen standing to a platform edge, and alongside a normal width rail vehicle, such as the Metro-Cammell DMU on the left in this picture of a new Class 141 taken at Huddersfield in the bay platform, on 12 July 1984. *John Chalcraft*

rated in the brake cylinder, so that when the vehicle is parked the brake will be applied as the air in the brake cylinder leaks off. The passenger emergency brake system is air operated by use of levers situated above the entrance doors in each vehicle. The stopping performance for the units is within the standard BR 'W' curve requirements at all speeds and loads.

The floor height of the vehicles is 1,285mm above the rail — slightly higher than the current multiple-unit standard of 1,157mm.

Writing in the February 1983 issue of *Modern Railways*, James Abbott analysed the attitude of the West and South Yorkshire Passenger Transport Executives *before* service experience with the Class 141; at that time envisaged as the replacement for the ageing 'classic' DMU fleet in that area, but not yet delivered. There was some dissatisfaction that neither PTE had been closely consulted during the design stages of the Class 141, and both reacted unfavourably to the internal layout of the units, as James Abbott reported:

'Both Executives are dismayed that such a high proportion of total floor space is devoted to the crew's requirements. The external doors which enable the crew to evacuate the unit in the event of violence without going through the passenger compartment are a particularly space-consuming feature of the 141 (and what, one wonders, is the innocent passenger supposed to do in such a situation?). Why should the guard have his own separate seat — why not let him occupy the driver's seat in the trailing cab? And why has there been no design provision for driver-only-operation, with passengers without tickets entering through a door next to a right-hand or centrally-placed driver? After all, it was re-equipment that prompted BR to force the pace of change in working practices on the St Pancras suburban services — why has not a similar opportunity been grasped in the case of the provincial services? Such questions appear doubly embarrassing to BR if comparison is made with current bus operating practices.

Above:
Now a familiar sight in West Yorkshire, the Class 141s are nevertheless questionable in terms of their sparse accommodation, and non-standard brake equipment which means that they cannot work in multiple, except with others of the same class. No set numbers are painted upon the ends now, and this example simply carries the class designation 141, the individual vehicle numbers now being used to identify them. Nearest the camera is No 55541, waiting on a Harrogate turn at York station on 8 November 1984.
Colin J. Marsden

'Another feature which the PTEs might have altered had the design of the Class 141 not been handed to them on a plate is the positioning of the external doors. Trials with the Class 140 prototype unit suggested a need for three passenger access doors on each side of a two-car unit, rather than the two in the 141.

141 units will have toilets (which the original R3 did not have), and both Executives endorse this feature. With vandalism prompting demolition of station toilets, on-train provision seems a reasonable course to follow.'

The South Yorkshire PTE also expressed concern over the potential riding qualities, after experience with the two axle R3 and the Class 140; again I quote James Abbott:

'While welcoming the concept of a four-wheeled vehicle with its inherently low capital cost (it is estimated that bogies add £30,000 to the cost of each car), SYPTE's chief reservation about such a unit concerns its riding qualities. Both the experimental R3 and the prototype Class 140 unit rode badly over jointed track (the 140 being particularly poor in this respect), with the continuous nodding motion tending to induce neck-ache on a long journey. Although some design improvements have been made to the 141, SYPTE is still apprehensive; but fortunately, much of the route-mileage in South Yorkshire is laid with continuous welded rail. However, BR might consider low-cost welding of jointed track, say every four or five consecutive joints, in order to improve the ride-quality of four-wheel units, especially on the poor quality track found on rural lines. Apart from improving the ride such a measure would reduce in-vehicle noise and would cut down on vehicle and track maintenance costs.'

Thus, even before a single Class 141 had turned a wheel in PTE service there were doubts and criticisms of its suitability! Some of these points were to prove valid, and some not so bad as feared, but the fact remains that the Class 141 did not come up to full requirement as a DMU for the future; in particular because of cramped passenger accommodation within the bus-width body, and in riding. The mechanical portions have also proved troublesome in service, and the class has not established a very good reliability record. What it also did *not* do was introduce a note of modernity and comfort; rather more one of sparse utility and cost-cutting; as one observer at the Press demonstration put it: 'It would have been cheaper to build a bus'!

It was at this stage that the mooted alternative of building a new fleet of 'classic' bogie DMUs really began to surface, and the Class 141 was destined to remain a 'one-off' fleet of 20 units; in some respects (including the two-pipe air-braking system) non-standard, and thus non-compatible with the new generation fleet. An idea which was canvassed was to withdraw them from BR service, refurbish them, and sell them overseas; replacing them with later designs of railcar or railbus (Classes 142, 143, 150 for example). Instead it has been decided to refurbish and modify these troublesome vehicles to bring them up to scratch and to make them compatible with the Classes 150/1, 142, 143, 144 which have the EP (electro-pneumatic) brake and BSI couplers including the electrical jumpers, now the standard for the future.

Sprinters, Pacers and Skippers: The New Generation DMUs

By the start of 1984 one of the two BR contenders for the new generation DMU fleet was quite firmly out of the running because it was too good! As Peter Kelly had earlier written in *Rail Enthusiast*, after the Class 210 DEMU was demonstrated to the press: 'Comparing it with Britain's only other type of DEMU, the much-loved Hastings units, is like comparing a Model T Ford with a Jaguar XJS'. He also observed that it was 'the best diesel multiple-unit-type train I have ever travelled on. And that might just be the problem: it could be *too* good!' Prophecy indeed, and what irony too! Price alone ruled against the Class 210.

On the other hand as just discussed, the Class 141 two-car railbus, although a vast improvement in many respects over the solitary Class 140 prototype, also had its critics, who were not enamoured by the narrow body and consequent seating restriction to 2+2. In this respect the first generation DMU fleet designs were considerably more generous to their passengers in available space and legroom. There was a lobby amongst the most interested parties for a new version of the 'classic' DMU; with the firm of Metro-Cammell showing interest as designers and builders. Such a DMU would be considerably cheaper than the Class 210, and potentially considerably more comfortable for the longer routes, than the four-wheeled Class 141, because it would be carried on modern four-wheel bogies, and would have more seating and space within; being built to normal BR loading gauge dimensions.

The indefatigable Roger Ford took up the story again, in the March 1984 issue of *Modern Railways* in an article entitled 'DMU replacement — can BR ever get it right?'. The reader will recall that in 1981 Roger Ford had ended his article (see page 37) by asking the question: 'Perhaps the only DMU replacement is another DMU?' I take up the story again at this point, where in a piece of the 1984 *Modern Railways* article, sub-headed: 'Rebirth of the classic DMU', Ford wrote that the idea of building a new generation of 'classic' DMUs lay fallow until a Railbus Conference which was held in November 1981. I quote:

'. . . This idea lay fallow until the railbus conference, when it became clear that a modern classic DMU was what the metropolitan counties really wanted. Leading the charge was West Midlands PTE, which not only needed to replace its existing DMU fleet but had, as a major employer within its area, Britain's only private-sector passenger railway vehicle builder, Metro-Cammell.

Below:
Interior view showing the passenger accommodation of the prototype Class 150 'Sprinter' design. No first class seating was provided in the Class 150 design. *British Rail*

Met-Cam had, of course, built many of BR's existing DMUs plus a smaller number for export in the 1970s. The company had done some work on a new generation DMU which it believed would provide a cost-effective replacement on higher density urban and inter-urban services. Key features of the design were, and are, one large diesel engine driving both axles on one bogie, giving reduced capital and maintenance cost and higher performance than classic DMUs, and alloy construction which, together with higher availability, increases capacity allowing three modern DMUs to do the work of four existing designs. Cost per seat was forecast to be marginally less than the Class 141 and about 75% that of a Class 210.

The proposal was perfectly timed. BR was starting to establish an arm's length relationship with BREL and the Government was particularly keen on opening up the nationalised industries to private sector competition. As a result, in March 1983, BREL and Metro-Cammell were each awarded a contract to build two, three-car, diesel multiple-unit trains for suburban, medium-density local and cross-country services. As the BR press release explained 'Each of the builders will be free to develop their own ideas to meet a common business specification to be subject only to certain technical performance requirements. This will enable a *comprehensive evaluation* of various engine and transmission systems, seating arrangements and other design facets to be made'.

One could be forgiven for thinking that the decision to go ahead with prototype development for a new generation of 'classic' diesel-mechanicals, would cast shadows upon the future of the bus-bodied two-axle railbus. The Sprinters — as the Class 150/151 have become known — could certainly do *all* the jobs that the Pacers and Skippers (as the Class 142/143 railbuses have recently been dubbed) could do; plus a lot more besides! However, BREL and Leyland were not deterred, and indeed pushed ahead with plans for a wide-bodied version (Class 142), having realised the limitations of the Class 141 very rapidly. Not only that. It was decided by British Rail to put out to tender for their design and construction to create competition within the market, with an eye to cutting initial purchase price. Thus the firms of Metro-Cammell, Marshalls of Cambridge and Walter Alexander (all in the bus-building business) were invited to become involved in the project. It was at this stage that the feasibility of fitting full rail-gauge width bodies seems to have emerged; whilst of course every contender had to satisfy BR with regard to the critical factor

Engine and transmission, class 150/1 trains

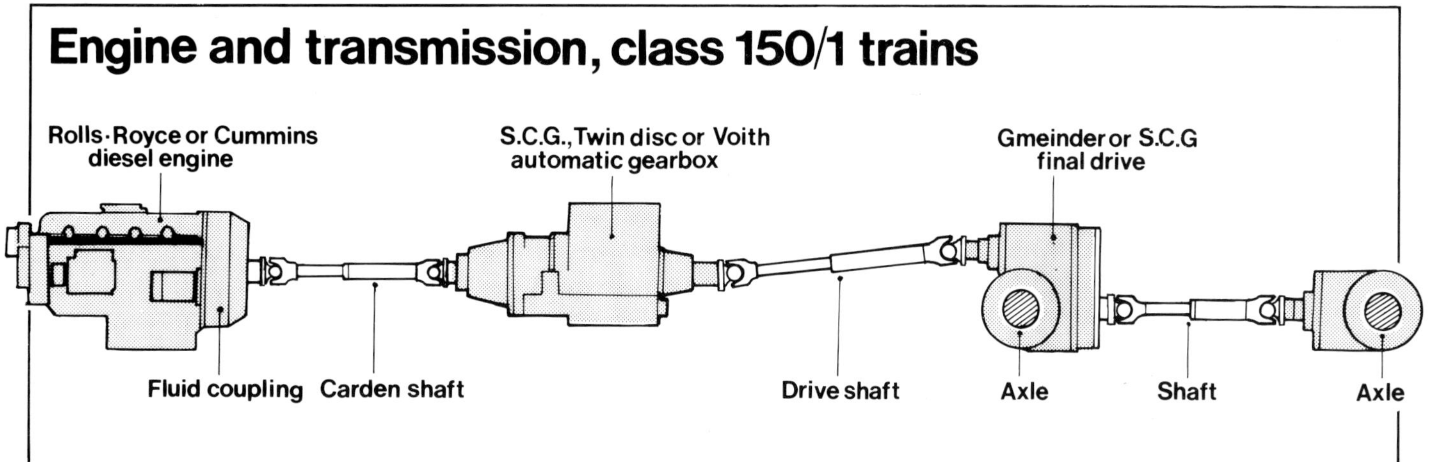

for railbuses — that of end-loadings, which had to meet strength requirements for safety reasons. There was a certain degree of freedom for the styling of the railbus; in particular of the front end.

All that is water under the bridge now, of course, because the Sprinters and Pacers and Skippers all appeared in service within months of each other. Not only that, but bulk orders were soon placed for more Class 150s and Classes 142/143 (see table) leaving only the Class 151 in what could be described as prototype form, awaiting its fate. A change to two-car formation instead of three-car has been made for the first production-build of Class 150/1, produced by BREL York, but otherwise they closely follow the form of the prototypes except for a livery modification (see illustrations). However, there are more changes to come, with the further batches now authorised (see table overleaf) in order to suit the requirements of the Provincial Services Sector, BR. In particular some of the new vehicles will be 23m long and will have 2+2 seating, in order to give greater comfort and amenity to Provincial Services of the longer duration runs across country. Gangways will be put into front ends once again to give more flexibility of working, and allow on-board ticket control and refreshment trolley services throughout the length of a multiple-unit formation.

Just as this manuscript was going to press, the BRB Provincial Services Sector Manager, Mr John Edmonds, announced plans for a new generation of 'Super-Sprinter' trains to cater for cross-country routes. These will be to higher standards of amenity and comfort, akin to InterCity carriages, and will be *faster* (100mph max) for use on services linking Brighton, Swansea, Bristol, Salisbury, and Liverpool and Scarborough.

By May 1986 more than 550 Sprinters and 288 Pacers had already been ordered at a cost of £200 million, and 400 more units are planned at an additional £100 million. Because the new generation units are more reliable and have longer maintenance cycles than the old fleet they are replacing, the fleet size will be cut by a third by 1991.

Never before has the DMU image been so bright on BR!

Top:
Explanation of the engine and transmission layout for the Class 150/1 Sprinter DMUs.

Above:
On Saturday 14 September 1985, the second Class 151 set was photographed at Idridgehay on the freight-only line between Duffield and Wirksworth, whilst working the 16.15 Wirksworth-Derby special. This train was operated in conjunction with the Wirksworth Festival. *C. J. Tuffs*

Below:
Class 142 two-car railbus No 142001, finished in brown/orange/white Manchester colours, is seen here at Bedford during trial running, on 10 June 1985. The rail-gauge width body and restyled front have resulted in an attractive new design — far less reminiscent of road vehicle practice, and certainly more modern in style than either the Class 140 or 141! *Alec Swain*

Sprinter 150

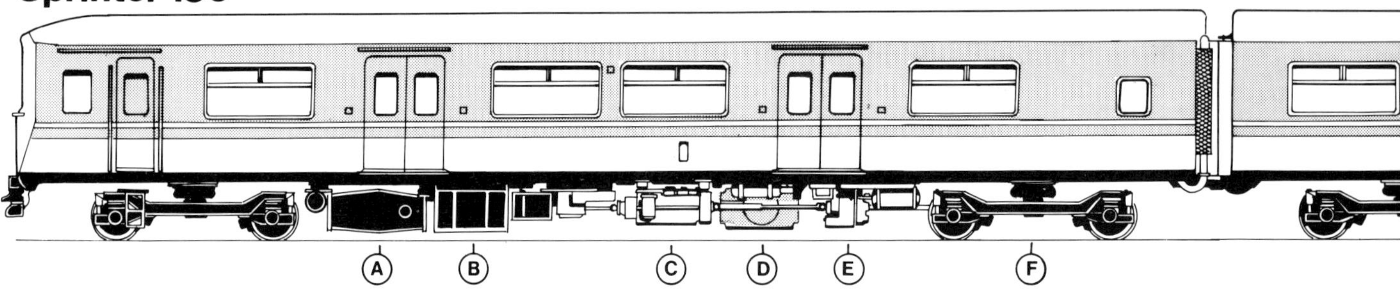

Sprinter Mediumweight DMUs

	Class 150/1	*Class 150/2*	*Class 155*	*Class 156*
Number of vehicles	100 (*50 2-car sets*)	170 (*85 2-car sets*)	70 (*35 2-car sets*)	228 (*114 2-car sets*)
Approximate value	£24.5m		£125m total	
Builder	BREL	BREL	Leyland Vehicles	Metro-Cammell
Date authorised	10 February 1984	15 January 1985	15 January 1985	30 October 1985
Date due in service	May 1986	1986-87	1987-88	1987-88

Notes:
Class 150/1: 20m long. 138 seats per set, arranged 3+2. Gangwayed within set. For use in East Midlands, Mid and North Wales.
Class 150/2: 20m long. 148 seats per set, arranged 3+2. Through gangways. For use on suburban and provincial services.
Class 155: 23m long. 160 seats per set, arranged 2+2 with armrests. Through gangways. For use on longer distance, cross-country services, eg Birmingham-Norwich.
Class 156: 23m long. 160 seats per set, arranged 2+2 with armrests. Through gangways. For use on longer distance, cross-country services.
Liveries:
All Sprinter units light blue above waist, grey beneath, white/blue stripes along waist.
Engines:
All production Sprinters powered by Cummins engines with Voith transmission and Gmeinder final drive.

Above:
The smart new face of the second generation DMUs is typified by prototype 'Sprinter' Class 150 No 150001, seen just after completion at BREL York works in 1984. The production series 'Sprinter' units are in two-car formation rather than the three-car layout seen here. *British Rail*

Left:
Undeniably handsome! The Class 143 'Pacers' produced by W. Alexander & Sons have an extremely well-designed front end, and more closely resemble railway vehicle styling practice than their Leyland cousins. Finished in Provincial Services Sector two tone blue and white, the first of the production batch of Class 143 (with underframes and running gear furnished by Andrew Barclay of Kilmarnock) No 143001 is seen on a demonstration run to Matlock Bath from Derby on 18 October 1985. *Peter Gater*

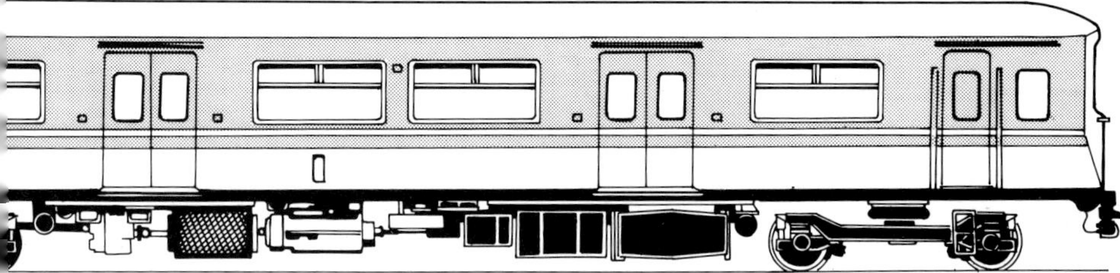

Left and below:
The principal actors featured in the new stage of BR traction development: The Sprinter Class 150 and the Class 142 and 143 Pacers.
A Fuel tank
B Battery and fuse box
C Diesel engine
D Radiator
E Automatic Gearbox
F Final drive or drives
David Gibbons

Pacer Lightweight 4-wheel Railbuses (called Skippers in the West Country)

	Class 141	*Class 142*	*Class 143*	*Class 142/1*	*Class 144*
Number of vehicles	40 *(20 2-car sets)*	100 *(50 2-car sets)*	50 *(25 2-car sets)*	92 *(46 3-car sets)*	46 *(23 2-car sets)*
Approximate value	£7m	£24m		£24m	
Builder	BREL/Leyland	ART (BREL/Leyland)	Alexander/Barclay	ART (BREL/Leyland)	Alexander/BREL
Date authorised		16 January 1984	16 January 1984	7 October 1985	7 October 1985
Date due in service	1983	Oct 1985-May 1986	Jan 1986-May 1986	1986-87	1986-87

Notes:
Class 141: Narrow body. 94 seats per set, arranged 2+2. For use on services in West Yorkshire.
Class 142: Wide body. 121 seats per set, arranged 2+2. For services in Greater Manchester, the Wirral and the West Country.
Class 143: Wide body. 122 seats per set, arranged 2+2. For services on Tyneside, including Tyne & Wear PTE.
Class 142/1: Wide body. 121 seats per set, arranged 2+2. For services in West Yorkshire and the North-West.
Class 144: Wide body. 122 seats per set, arranged 2+2. For services in West Yorkshire and Humberside.
Liveries:
Most Pacers are painted in similar colours to the Sprinters, but blue beneath the waist, with the following exceptions.
Class 141: All in West Yorkshire PTE green and cream.
Class 142: West Country Skipper units in brown and cream. Some in Greater Manchester PTE orange and brown.
Class 143: Six units in Tyne & Wear PTE yellow and white.
Class 142/1: Some in Greater Manchester PTE orange and brown.
Class 144: Some in West Yorkshire PTE red and buttermilk.
Engines:
All Pacers and Skippers powered by Leyland engines with SCG transmission and final drive.

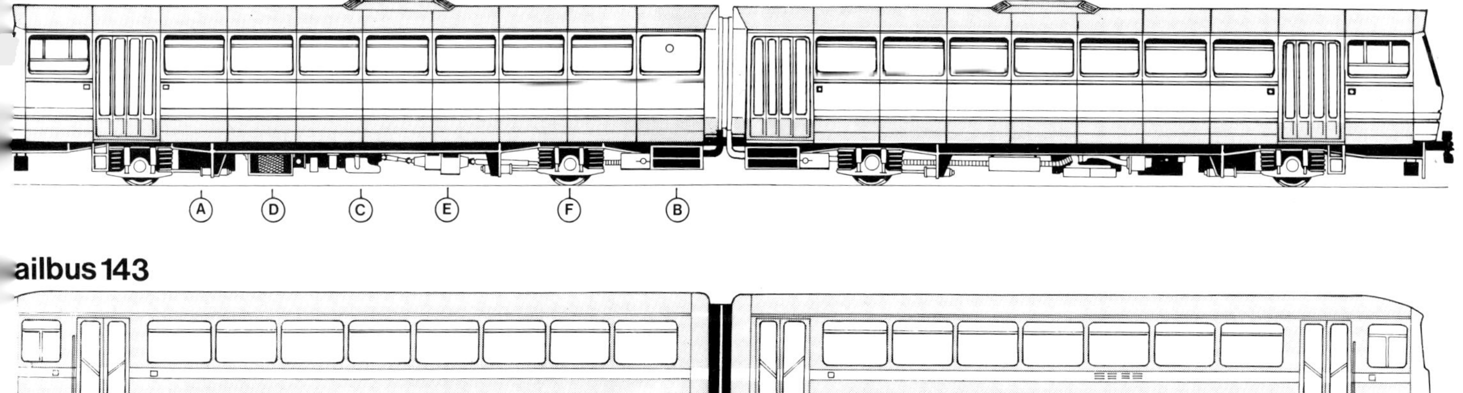

8 York Works BREL. General Purpose Prototypes 3-Car. Class 150

Introduced: 1984
Purpose: General duties, ranging from commuter services to cross-country and secondary main line services
No of Cars per unit: 3*
TOPS Class: 150
Engines: Cummins NT 855R5†/Rolls-Royce 'Eagle' C6280HR‡
Horsepower: 855†/840‡
Transmission: Mechanical. Voith†/SCG‡
Body: 19.93m×2.73m
Unit Nos: 150001†/150002‡
Brake Type: Air, twin pipe
Maximum speed: 75mph
Coupling restrictions: With units of same class; also Class 151
Original Running Nos/Vehicle Type/ Weight: 55200†/55201‡ DMS, 35.4 tonnes
55300†/55301‡, DMS, 34.7 tonnes
55400†/1‡. MS, 35 tonnes

Notes: *The above details relate only to the two 3-car prototype sets. Later builds are of two-car formation, with Cummins/ Voith power equipment. Units are gangwayed within, but not at driving ends.
‡This unit is being modified as Class 154 prototype.

The contract for two prototype three-car diesel multiple-unit trains was placed with BREL in March 1983 — a similar contract also going to Metro-Cammell on that date. Two quite different designs were planned to permit evaluation prior to finalising the future DMU. The Derby/BREL design, based upon the Mk 3 coach, became known as the Class 150, and the Metro-Cammell the Class 151, (see next Section). Aided by the fact that York works was already tooled-up for Mk 3 EMU production, BREL actually completed the first Class 150 three months ahead of schedule, and it was handed over to BR Provincial Services Sector on 8 June 1984; with the second following soon afterwards. The two BREL prototypes each comprised three vehicles, gangwayed only within the set; a factor which allowed some smartening-up of the front end design, compared to the Class 210 (see Section 6); although there is now some talk of putting front end gangways back on future builds — C'est la vie!

Each of the two BREL Class 150 prototypes comprises three vehicles, and has a different power equipment package for evaluation purposes. All vehicles are powered, and driving cabs are fitted in the outer end of each three-car set. Up to four units can be coupled together to operate in multiple; and the vehicles are designed to be compatible with Class 151. Maximum design speed of the prototype units is 75mph (120km/h).

Bodyside construction incorporates IZ steel skin and IZ rails and pillars, joined using resistance spot welding. The small heat input involved in this technique minimises distortion. The roof is corrugated mild steel and does not employ purlins.

The structure can withstand 150 tonnes at coupler level and meets all International Union of Railways (UIC) end-load requirements. The vehicle is designed for a 30 year fatigue life, and the driving cars weigh approximately 35 tonnes in working order.

Sound insulation is ensured by the use of an anti-drumming compound which is applied as a spray within the body structure. This is supplemented by fibreglass thermal and acoustic insulation in the bodyside floor and roof. Bogie design also reduces the level of track sound transmitted to the passenger saloons.

The first unit is powered by a Cummins NT-855-R5 engine rated at 285hp (213kW) at 2,100rpm, driving a Voith 211 hydraulic transmission via a cardan shaft. Gmeinder final drive assemblies are provided. This combination has a successful history of operation in the Netherlands but whether any lessons can be learnt from this for application to operation on Britain's often steeply-graded branch lines had to be ascertained.

The second unit has a Rolls-Royce Eagle C6 280 HR engine rated at 280hp. This drives a Self Changing Gears R500 fully automatic gearbox via a cardan shaft. The final drive assemblies are also supplied by SCG. Auxiliary power is supplied by two alternators driven by a splitter gearbox from the engine.

Bogies are developed from the successful BT13 family. Secondary suspension is by air-bags, and incorporates a levelling valve for maintaining standard floor height. Air operated tread brakes using composition blocks are fitted. The system incorporates SAB cylinders and slack adjusters.

Fully automatic BSI couplers are fitted instead of Tightlock couplers at the outer ends of the driving vehicles, enabling units to be coupled and uncoupled (including pneumatic and electrical systems) without the need for shunting staff to go between the vehicles. Within each set the cars are linked by semi-permanent bar couplers.

The passenger accommodation of the Class 150 DMU bears close resemblance to its Class 455 EMU sisters. Every vehicle has two double sliding doors each side for passenger use, but there are no obstructive grab poles as in the 455s. The doors are under the control of the guard but can be transferred to passenger operation; there are also controls for driver operation of doors. There is an 'emergency open' system for each door — a notable departure by comparison with Class 455

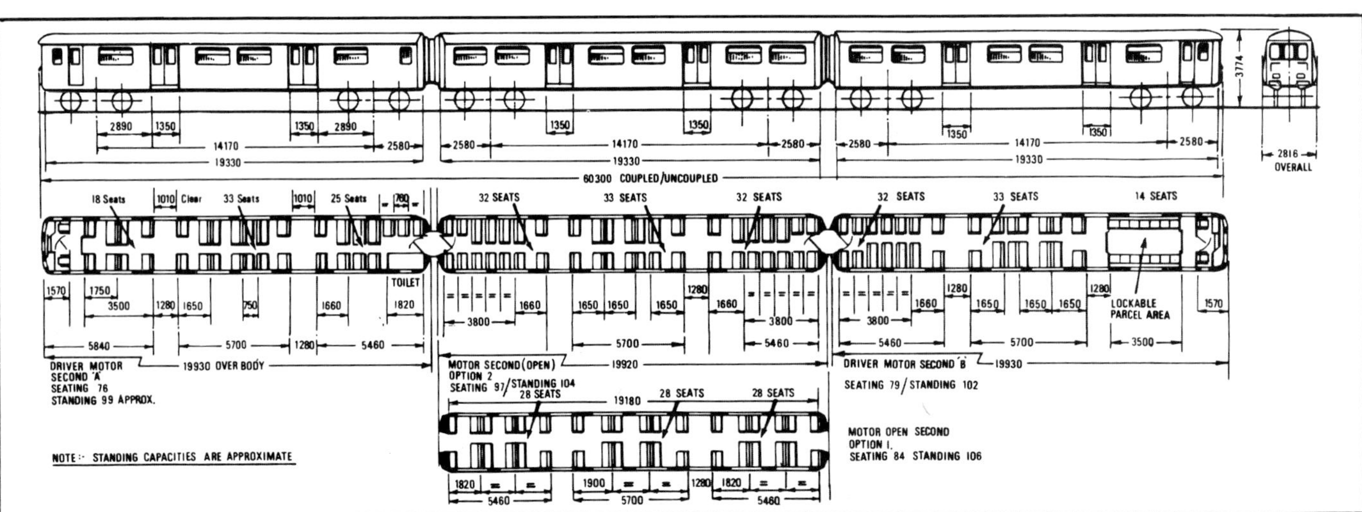

Below:
Elevation and plan of prototype three-car Class 150 Sprinter designed and built by BREL; showing alternative seat layouts for the centre vehicle.

and 317 EMUs, where it seems that in the event of an accident passengers are expected to troop out of the train ends, via the gangway connection door.

Double-glazed window units are fitted, incorporating tinted glass to reduce glare and condensation.

The heating system uses waste heat from the engines. Heating units are mounted under the seats, and warm air distribution is assisted by fans. The system is supplemented by an oil-fired water heater, which also acts as an engine pre-heater. Ventilators are incorporated in the roof, and air circulation is further aided by hinged twin-hopper windows during warm weather.

Lighting is by undiffused 4ft fluorescent tubes placed longitudinally in each vehicle.

Passenger gangways affording full access between cars are provided within each set. Although connections are not fitted in the end cabs for access between adjacent units, the design is adaptable to provide this facility at a later date if required which in fact as already stated, now seems likely. In this case the Class 455 layout would probably be used, in its most recent form without the roof box above the cab which featured on the Class 210/317 and early batch of Class 455.

Seating saloons are segregated from the doorway vestibules — which are slightly narrower than on 455s, though the door width is the same — by draught screens incorporating toughened glass. A notable improvement by comparison with Class 455s is that a lockable parcels area is

Top:
Prototype Sprinter No 150001 is seen in the pleasing surroundings of Matlock station on 4 January 1985, waiting to work the 13.12 service to Derby. *L. A. Nixon*

Above:
It was eventually decided to build the first production order for Class 150 Sprinters as two-car sets. During evaluation trials to establish the suitability of the design for use on the Cambrian and Central Wales lines and elsewhere, the prototype No 150001 sometimes ran with the centre vehicle removed; as a two-car set. It is seen here passing University station (Birmingham) while undergoing trials on the Lichfield-Bromsgrove cross-city line; another future role for the new Sprinter. *Geoff Dowling*

provided in one vehicle of each set, with tip-up seats fitted to give extra passenger accommodation during times of heavy traffic.

The prototype trains feature two different types of seats in the main saloons. The first unit is fitted throughout with bus-type seats and includes a mix of unidirectional seating and facing bays. Seating capacity is 252 with a crush loading capacity of 617. The non-driving vehicle of the second unit has BR's standard inner-suburban seating similar to that used on the Southern Region Class 455 electric units. This gives a seating capacity for the unit of 239. All seats are fitted with removable covers for ease of cleaning and maintenance.

The design, however, is sufficiently flexible to accept a wide range of alternative seating from bench seats to InterCity standard, and the ratio of seats to standing space can be varied to suit individual operating requirements.

A modular toilet compartment is fitted on one vehicle of each unit incorporating flush toilet and washing facilities.

The layout of the driver's cab is similar to that used on other recent multiple-unit trains, and incorporates a wheelslip detection device. Automatic sliding doors give crew access via transverse vestibules adjacent to the cab. The cab therefore has no external doors, eliminating draughts. However, one drawback to this layout is that the transverse vestibules take up valuable potential seating space; British Rail's Provincial Services Director John Edmonds said at the time of their introduction that he would be seeking union agreement to a Tyne & Wear Metro-style cab, with seats going right up to the front windows on the offside for future builds; though this remains doubtful for safety reasons. Cab to cab communication and a public address system are fitted and provision exists to install train-to-signalbox radio at a later date if required.

The prototype Class 150 units were allocated to Derby Etches Park depot and ran extensive trials on the regular passenger service between Derby and Matlock, on what became known as the 'Sprinter-Link', the sets themselves being named Sprinters — a name which has been in use for some time on the continent, Holland in particular — to describe multiple-units with fast acceleration. By November 1984 their performance was considered so impressive that the go-ahead was given to build a further 50 sets, but as two-car rather than three-car formations. From May 1986 it was planned to have virtually all DMU services in the East Midlands and North and Mid-Wales operated by these Sprinters built at York by BREL. The order was worth £22 million.

In 1986 the new Sprinters took over most services on the Crewe-Birmingham-Derby-Nottingham-Lincoln-Grantham axis, also on the Birmingham-Leicester and Derby-Matlock services. They will also be the mainstay of a new direct service between Nottingham and Sheffield. In Wales they are taking over the local runs between the North Wales Coast and Crewe and Manchester, together with services from Crewe and Chester to Shrewsbury and on the Cambrian Coast lines to Aberystwyth and Pwhllei, where they are a major factor in a complete modernisation of the line, which includes radio signalling. Livery for the new units is the Provincial Services two-tone blue/white/light grey.

During trials on the Derby-Matlock services the prototypes covered the trip in 21min compared to the usual journey time of 32min; whilst overnight trial runs between Derby and London, St Pancras were undertaken in 110min. Introduction of the Sprinters meant that by May 1986 almost all East Midlands services were operated either by HSTs or Sprinters — the first part of the BR network to be completely modernised in this way.

Early in 1985 it was announced that Government approval had been given for the construction of a further 240 Sprinter vehicles; to replace 385 existing DMU vehicles, all over 20 years old. The Sprinters are expected to cost around £60 million. At the time of this announcement, Mr John Edmonds, BR's Director, Provincial Services said: 'With delivery of these new vehicles we shall be able to make a real start on our local train replacement programme aimed at giving better value to our passengers and the tax payer'. The vehicles are likely to be operated on services in the Bristol area, the Cardiff Valleys, West Wales, Lincolnshire, parts of Scotland (including the new service for Bathgate from 1986) and in several of the major city conurbations — including non-electrified routes in the West Midlands and Greater Manchester.

Some of this order will be for the existing 20m-long Class 150 design and some for a new 23m-long version. The WR, in particular seems prepared to spend money improving loading gauge clearances, in the Cardiff Valleys in particular, in order to be able to run the longer version. Another area of doubt has been the suitability of the existing Sprinter design for the longer InterCity feeder routes such as Crewe-Portsmouth; Oxford-Worcester-Hereford; Bristol-Taunton and West Wales, etc. For these services a 90-100mph top speed is desirable, and four-coach layouts. This requirement will see a further version of the class designed and produced; dubbed already the 'Super-Sprinters'.

Above right:
The effective headlights fitted to the Sprinters are well demonstrated in this view of No 150001 at Derby on the night of 20 February 1985. Good visual warning is highly important on provincial routes, with their plethora of public right of way level crossings and farmland accommodation crossings. *Colin J. Marsden*

Right:
Testing of the 'Sprinter' prototypes has been very thorough, and these precursors of the 'New Generation' fleet have happily shown a considerable advance in design, comfort, acceleration and riding over the traditional DMUs which they are destined to replace. During February 1986, unit No 150001 took part in trials on the Fort William and Oban routes, and was photographed arriving at Ardlui on 17 February with the 09.50 Glasgow-Fort William. *T. H. Noble*

9 Metro-Cammell. General Purpose Prototypes 3-Car. Class 151

Introduced: 1985
Purpose: General duties; mainly suburban, for evaluation
No of Cars per Unit: 3
TOPS Class: 151
Engines: Cummins NT 855R5
Horsepower: 855
Transmission: Hydro-mechanical
Body: —
Unit Nos: 151001-151002
Brake Type; Air, twin pipe
Maximum speed: 75mph
Coupling restrictions: With units of same class; also Class 150/0
Original Running Nos/Vehicle Type/ Weight: 55202/3, DMS(L), 34.3 tonnes. 55402/3, MS, 32.7 tonnes, 55302/3, DMS, 33.3 tonnes

Notes: Heating is by waste heat recovery warm air ducting.

Possibly at the time the most stylish DMU ever to take to British rails, the Metro-Cammell Class 151 prototypes were unfortunately late in delivery (whereas the BREL Class 150 was early) and before completion the builders encountered some problems with the railway trade unions over the design and layout of the driver/guard accommodation. Delays whilst changes were made, meant that the first Class 151 did not take to the rails until February 1985; meanwhile fleet building of the rival Class 150 of BREL had already begun — despite lack of time to test and compare the two alternative prototypes. To some extent this was due to the urgent need to replace existing asbestos-contaminated 'classic' BR DMUs. The replacement programme quickly gathered pace, and in 1985 the Government authorised a further 240 Sprinters, but not of the Metro-Cammell design, and it became evident that the Class 151 was already out-of-the running for further Sprinter orders. Instead Metro-Cammell will be involved in the design and construction of the new (23m) longer type, with gangwayed ends. Viewed against this early rejection of the class for production it remains to be said that in some respects the Class 151 is a superior design to its BREL Class 150 rival, in particular in the layout of the seats and bodyside windows (compare illustrations, and it is evident that the Class 151 offers much better natural illumination, and lineside views to each seating bay). The technical details of the aluminium-bodied Class 151 — still only in prototype form of two three-car sets are as follows:

Each car is carried on two four-wheel bogies by an air bag-type secondary suspension. A primary suspension unit comprising rubber chevrons is provided at each axle box. It is debatable if this type of bogie is as versatile as the BREL version; in particular in the higher speed ranges, but it is well-proven for suburban-type duties. Each car has both axles of one of its bogies powered, and the three cars of each unit are coupled by semi-permanent bar-type couplers, with gangways between vehicles within the set, but not at the driving ends. Access to the passenger compartment is by two pairs of pneumatically-operated sliding leaf doors on each car side. The door control circuit and interlocks provide for the following:

A One-man operation.
B Two-man operation.
C Circuit initiation by train staff with passengers operating local pushbuttons to open and close doors with staff control over door closing.
D Staff control only.

Each car is fitted with an underframe-mounted horizontal turbo-charged six-

Below:
In many respects the most stylish DMU ever to run in Britain, the Metro-Cammell Class 151 Sprinter sets a new fashion in front end design and livery; with unpainted alloy finishes playing a prominent role. No 151001 is seen on 3 September 1985 at Matlock station before departure as the 17.17 to Derby. *Peter Marsh*

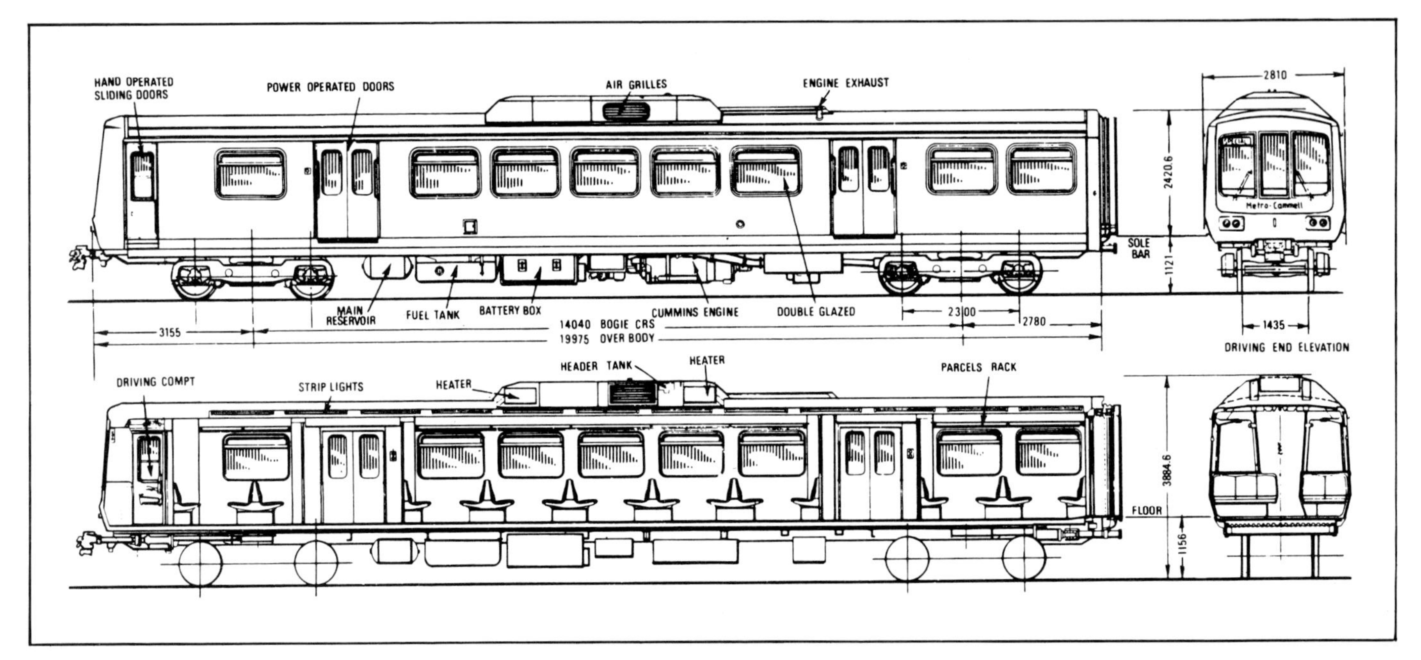
HAND OPERATED SLIDING DOORS
POWER OPERATED DOORS
AIR GRILLES
ENGINE EXHAUST
2810
2420.6
Metro-Cammell
SOLE BAR
1121
MAIN RESERVOIR
FUEL TANK
BATTERY BOX
CUMMINS ENGINE
DOUBLE GLAZED
2300
2780
3155
14040 BOGIE CRS
19975 OVER BODY
1435
DRIVING END ELEVATION
DRIVING COMPT
STRIP LIGHTS
HEATER
HEADER TANK
HEATER
PARCELS RACK
3884.6
FLOOR
1156

Left:
The highly individual modern styling of the Metro-Cammell Class 151 design is evident in this side view of DMS(L) No 55202 of unit 151001 at Derby. The bogies have Metalistic rubber primary suspension and air-bag secondary suspension. *Colin Boocock*

Above left:
Dimensions and layout of a driving motor second, power car for the Class 151 Metro-Cammell prototype three-car Sprinter.

Left:
Metro-Cammell prototype Class 151 Sprinter No 151001 is seen here being propelled along the Mickleover test line by Class 31 No 31327 on 25 February 1985, while being transferred from Derby Railway Technical Centre to Mickleover, for commissioning tests. The picture was taken at Etwall. The roof-mounted heaters and radiator units are prominent in this view. *C. J. Tuffs*

cylinder Cummins diesel engine. These are rated at 285bhp at 2,100rpm. The Cummins NT 855-R4 engine is fitted with the Cummins PT integrated fuel system.

The cooling system is of the 'make-up' type. The engine and radiators are connected in a closed circuit with a header tank positioned such that the minimum level in the tank will be above the highest point in the circuit. Bleed pipes from the engine and radiators to the header tank allow air to escape and a level switch in this tank protects against coolant loss. Coolant is topped up from an underframe-mounted reserve tank of 12gal connected to the header tank. This allows for re-filling of the header tank from the trackside by means of an electrically-driven pump mounted on the reserve tank.

The hydro-mechanical transmission consists of a single-stage hydro-kinetic torque-converter associated with a three-speed bi-directional 'hot shift' gearbox.

The converter drive is limited to the bottom ⅔rds of first gear so that the equipment combines the smooth starting and low speed accelerative attributes of hydraulic transmission with the efficiency of a close-ratio gearbox over the major portion of the vehicle speed range.

The single-stage torque converter with free-wheeling stator and automatic lock-up clutch is mounted directly on the engine flywheel housing. The converter lock-up operates at 25mph. The multiple layshaft gearbox is actuated by electro-hydraulic solenoid valves and facilitates choice of individual ratios without repercussions on adjacent gear steps.

The first gear torque multiplication permits the use of a high mechanical ratio and reduced steps between subsequent ratios. The transmission is designed for full throttle ('hot shift') gear change, eliminating pauses for engine speed die-down. Selection is by plate clutches and transmission is cushioned by momentary institution of the converter during transition. Reverse is also selected by plate clutches and a free wheel mode is effected by selection of neutral when the engine is returned to idle.

The connections between hydraulic torque converter and gearbox and final drives are by cardan shafts.

The hydrostatic drive consists of a variable displacement pump which provides oil to the hydraulic drive motors for the alternator, compressor and fan motor. The pump is driven by a shaft connected to the engine crankshaft nose and is self-controlled to give a near constant oil flow between minimum and maximum engine speed.

The oil from the pump is first fed to the alternator drive motor, which has a pressure relief valve connected in parallel to govern the oil pressure delivered to the alternator drive motor. This motor ensures an alternator speed of 2,650rpm at engine idling speed and 3,200rpm at maximum engine speed.

The oil then flows to the compressor drive motor which has a solenoid operated flow valve in parallel. The solenoid flow valve is activated by the air pressure in the main reservoir pipe to shut down the compressor when the required air pressure is available. The compressor speed varies between 1,850rpm and 2,300rpm depending upon engine speed. The system pump self-controls to limit its output as the demand from the various motors varies.

The oil finally flows to the fan motor which has a thermostatic fan controller in parallel. A thermostatic sensor in the engine coolant circuit restricts the by-pass valve in the controller such that, as the water temperature increases, the fan speed increases until full speed is attained. The reverse is also true: as the water temperature decreases the fan speed drops.

Each cab is fitted with a binary throttle controller, the design of which has been patented by the Westinghouse Brake & Signal Co. This operates on three binary coded train wires using seven switches. The controller operates the switches using cams in a way which precludes erroneous throttle wire energisation during transitions between steps. The code is used to operate four valves to give seven throttle steps plus engine idle.

The transmission is controlled by a micro-processor which ensures correct gear selection depending upon road speed.

The Class 151 is fitted with wheelslip detection equipment featuring automatic throttle dip.

The brake system is of the two pipe (brake pipe and main reservoir pipe) automatic type, being pneumatically controlled by a driver's brake controller and control unit at each driving position.

Each bogie is fitted with four brake actuators, two of which incorporate spring-applied parking brake cylinders. The parking brake actuators, like the other actuators, incorporate a pneumatic service brake cylinder.

The parking brake cylinder requires the application of air pressure to oppose the action of the spring and thus release the parking brake. Each actuator applies a double block holder with two composition blocks to the tread of each wheel.

The brake equipment on each car also employs a measurement of the vehicle air suspension pressure to modify the braking force applied in proportion to the vehicle load.

Class 151 DMUs can be multipled with the Class 150/0 prototype units. Up to three units can be operated in multiple, each unit consisting of two, three or four cars. In multiple operation the performance of the automatic air brake is reduced and must be taken into account.

The marshalling of units into trains is simplified by fully-automatic BSI couplers fitted to the outer ends of each unit. The coupler provides for mechanical, electrical and pneumatic coupling between units, thus eliminating the need for separate hose and jumper cables between units.

Non-driving power cars of different classes cannot be interchanged.

The heating of the saloon is by water from the engine cooling system. Incorpo-

Above:
No 151002 arrives at Duffield with the 11.05 Matlock-Derby on 12 September 1985.
I. J. Hodson

Left:
Interior view of the Class 151 Metro-Cammell DMU driver's cab showing the clean, simple layout of the control desk. *J. R. Dungate*

Above right:
The second of the two Metro-Cammell prototypes, No 151002 is seen in the Derby Railway Technical Centre yard during trials and evaluation. The dimensions of the vehicles are contrasted by the former Cravens parcels railcar (then a test vehicle) to the immediate right-hand background, and by the Mk 3 sleeping car on the left. *Colin J. Marsden*

rated into the system is an oil heater and pump unit to assist warm up.

When the water temperature is less than 50°C, the water circulation is restricted to the cab heater and engine, with the oil heater assisting warm up.

When the water temperature is above 50°C, coolant circulates through the engine, cab heater, floor heater and roof heater matrices. The oil heater continues to burn until the coolant temperature reaches 78°C. If the saloon temperature is below 18°C the floor fans run at full speed providing re-circulated heated air, with the roof fans switched off. If, however, the saloon temperature is in the range of

Above:
Restored to its three-car formation, No 151001 passes Stenson Junction on 7 January 1986, forming the 12.20 Crewe-Derby service. The roof-mounted air heating/cooling equipment is a very distinctive feature of this design. *A. O. Wynn*

18-21°C, the floor fans run at half speed and the roof fans run at half speed, thus introducing fresh air into the saloon.

When the saloon temperature is greater than 21°C, the roof fans run at full speed and coolant circulation to the floor and roof heaters is cut off until the saloon temperature drops to below 21°C again.

The communication equipment installed on each unit provides the following facilities:

A Broadcast messages to train passengers (public address mode).

B Communication between the driver and guard (cab/cab mode).

The equipment comprises a transmitting amplifier located in each cab, receiving amplifier located in each car and a system of loudspeakers installed in each car.

Provision has been made for the fitting of radio equipment at a later date, should it be required.

The layout of the Class 151 prototypes is as follows:

Vehicle Type	*Designation*	*Accommodation*
Driving power	DMS	Second class seats (80) Driving cab
Non-driving power car	MS	Second class seats (84)
Driving power car with baggage area and toilet	DMSBT	Second class seats (68). Baggage area. Toilet. Driving cab

Both Class 151 sets are in unpainted aluminium finish, with bold lining of the new two-tone blue and white of Provincial Services Sector.

10 British Leyland/BREL Derby. Local & Secondary Services 2-Car. Class 142

Introduced: 1985
Purpose: Local and Secondary services
No of Cars per Unit: 2
TOPS Class: 142
Engines: Leyland TL11 (2)
Horsepower: 410
Transmission: Mechanical SCG
Body: 15.66×2.8m
Unit Nos: 142001-142050
Brake Type: Electro-pneumatic
Max Unit Speed: 75mph
Coupling restrictions: With units of same class; also Classes 143, 144, 150/1, 150/2
Original Running Nos/Vehicle Type/ Weight:
55542-55591, DMS, 23.26 tonnes
55592-55641, DMS(L), 24.97 tonnes

Notes: Initial order for 50 2-car sets

THE British Rail Engineering/Leyland consortium, now known as Associated Rail Technologies (ART) did not rest upon its laurels once the Class 141 design had appeared. With an eye to the export market, a high density single-unit was produced (with 141-type front ends) and the design team developed a modification to the body modules which freed it from the bus-width restriction imposed by the existing jigs on the Leyland National production line at Workington. The Class 142 design did not, however, feature this wider body to begin with, and the plan was to build only the last 10 of any order gained as 'wide-body' railbuses. In the event, BR asked for, and got, all the Class 142s as 'wide-bodied', with no increase in price! This was undoubtedly due to the competitive bid by the firm of Walter Alexander (see Section 11) who were able to offer a wide-bodied design.

As a result of this, the Class 142 has provided the Provincial Services Sector and the PTEs, etc., with an extra seat per row (3+2) and this gives 121 second class seats, plus a toilet. This toilet is of modular construction developed by Leyland Bus, based on glass reinforced plastics panels with an integral washbasin and vanity unit. There is better use of space within the vehicle body, with a revised BR specification whereby the driver access door in the second bay (a feature of the Class 141s) is done away with in favour of a passenger access door. This could permit driver-only operation (DOO) at some future date. All the doors are power operated whereas the Class 141 has a pair of hinged doors behind the driver. The Class 142 two-car set is equipped with two Leyland 218hp turbocharged diesel engines, each driving one axle at the inner end through an SCG automatic gearbox and final drive unit.

The first order, for 50 Class 142 units costing around £350,000 apiece destined for the North West of England and Devon and Cornwall, has had no less than three different liveries applied:
14 in Manchester PTE colours of brown/orange/white
13 in Western Region 'chocolate and cream'. (known as 'Skippers')
23 in Provincial Services two-tone blue (for Manchester area).

In the autumn of 1985 ART received a follow-up order for a further 46 two-car sets — now called 'Pacers'.

There is no doubt that the adoption of the wider body (the Class 141 is 10in narrower) has produced a more economical and attractive package, and incidentally a safer one for passengers, because it reduces the gap at platform edges. Some improvement in front end styling has been achieved, and the Class 142 fits neatly into the 'new generation' BR DMU fleet, in appearance. It can run in multiple with Class 143 and the 'Sprinter' classes, but not with Class 141, due to the latter's brake system differences and to the use of the now standard BSI automatic coupler design instead of the Tightlock type fitted to Class 141. All three classes — 150, 142, 143 — have a maximum service speed of 75mph, even when in multiples of bogie/two axle vehicle formations.

As well as the home market, ART is much concerned to sell the Railbuses overseas, and one Class 142 vehicle was shipped to Belgium for exhibition during a Brussels conference in May 1985. After several shaky starts, the ART designers seem to have come up with a real winner!

Below:
Photographed at Bedford carriage sidings during trials on 10 June 1985, the first Class 142 railbus, No 142001 sets out on the return trial run to Derby. *Alec Swain*

No longer does the name Railbus conjure up images of cheap and cheerful transport; it now belongs more 'up-market', and with a bright future. Meanwhile the Western Region has disclosed its three phase plans for the complete replacement of the existing 'classic' DMU fleet and for the elimination of Mk 1 locomotive-hauled trains. The first phase of this plan involves the Class 142 railbuses, based on Plymouth Laira depot. This was implemented by May 1986, using the 13 new two-car sets working to a new timetable. Class 142 replaced traditional DMUs in Devon and Cornwall on local services from Exeter to Barnstaple, Exmouth and Honiton; on the Torquay branch, and on the Gunnislake, Looe, Newquay, Falmouth and St Ives services. The 13 Class 142s (26 vehicles) displaced 40 old vehicles, and fuel costs have been cut; a Class 142 being 20% more fuel efficient. The 'Pacers' may well be the salvation of a good many branch lines up and down the country — whose future would otherwise be bleak. In which case they have arrived on the scene just in time!

The long wheelbase of the Class 142 units led in the South-west to persistent problems with flange wear on sharp curves, together with associated noise and damage to the track. As a result, during 1986 within a short time of their introduction, the Class 142s were temporarily taken off the St Ives, Looe and Gunnislake branches, pending a solution. Proposals were put forward to fit the units with wheel flange lubrication, together with traditional sanding equipment. In the meantime these services were entrusted to the familiar 'First Generation' bogie DMUs.

In September 1986 the first Class 142/1 unit entered service. The new units were almost identical with the first 50 members of Class 142 and were numbered in sequence with them (see Section 14, page 77).

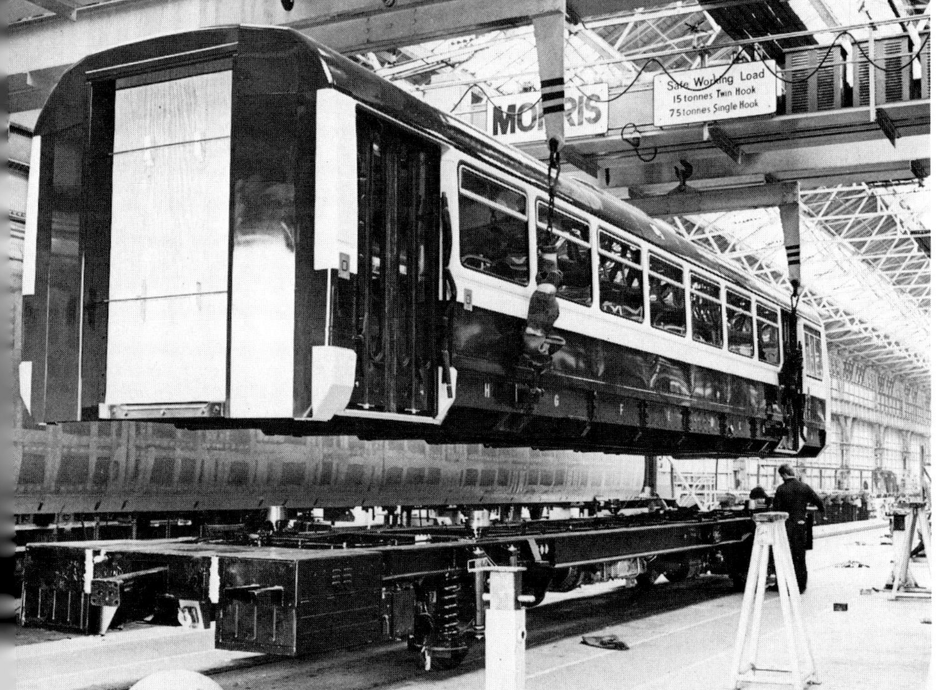

Above:
When is a bus not a bus? Answer: When it becomes a train! Here we see the Class 142 bus body, constructed by the Workington Leyland Bus Works arriving by road at BREL's Derby Litchurch Lane Works. The body is already painted in Devon & Cornwall brown and cream livery. Sitting upon the road vehicle's low-loader it looks far more like a bus than a train — thereby disclosing its true origins! *Colin J. Marsden*

Left:
Road technology and rail technology are then married together. Pictured here is a Class 142 Leyland railbus body being lowered on to a BREL-produced rail chassis in the Derby Litchurch Lane workshops on 30 September 1985. *Colin J. Marsden*

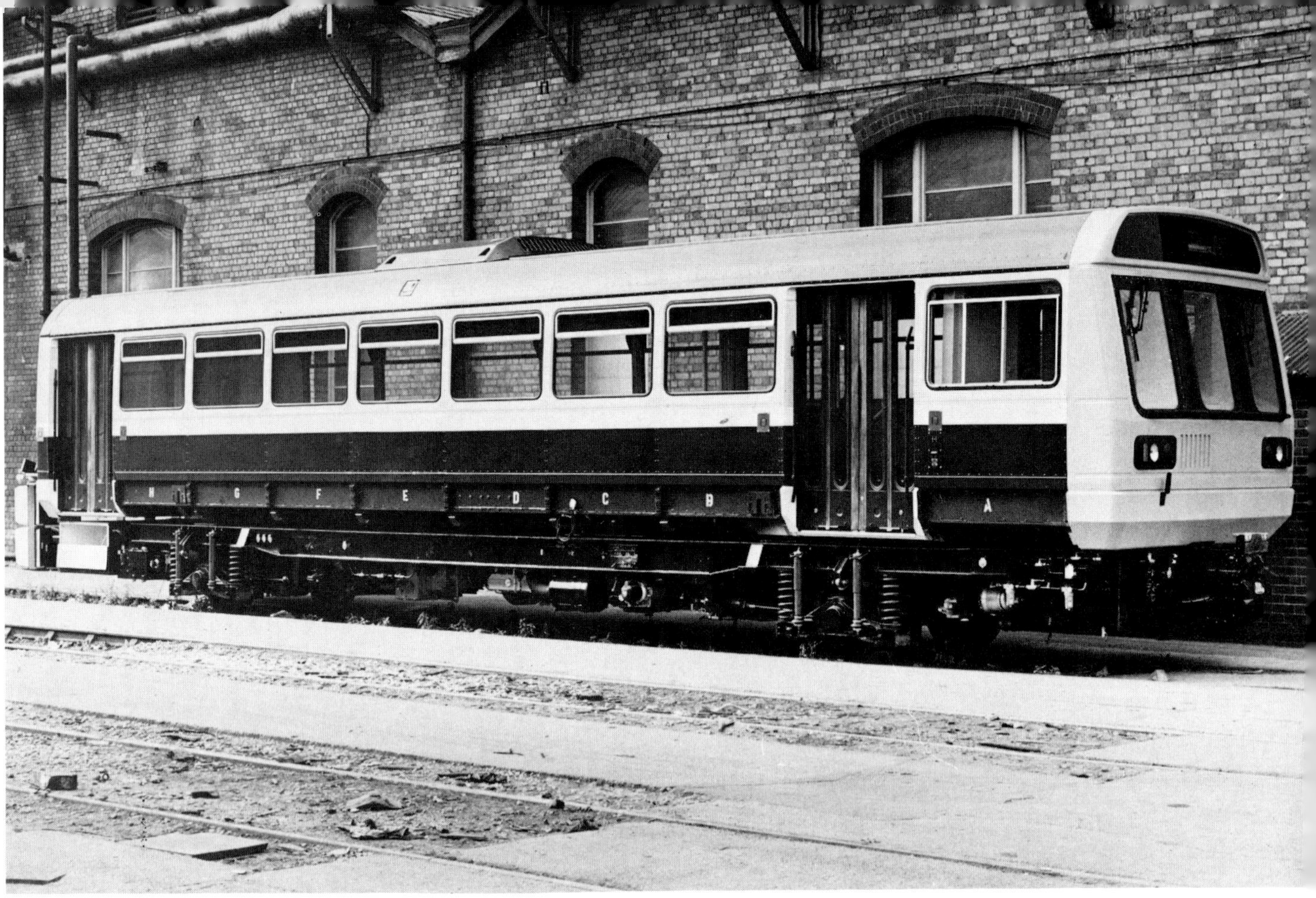

Above:
Finished in Devon & Cornwall 'Skipper' brown and cream livery, a Class 142 vehicle stands at Derby Litchurch Lane; awaiting fitting-out, on 30 September 1985. Lower portions of body panelling are not yet fitted and the rail underframe is clearly visible. *Colin J. Marsden*

Left:
Ready for service! A Western Region 'Skipper' Class 142, No 142015, in brown and cream livery. From May 1986 onwards they have formed the backbone of local services within Devon and Cornwall, replacing ageing diesel multiple-units dating from the 1950s.
British Rail

Below left:
Western Region 'Skipper' No 142019 stands in the branch bay platform at Liskeard on 9 April 1986, awaiting departure as the 10.57 to Looe. *David Percival*

Above right:
Nos 142019 and 142016 leave Exmouth with the 18.15 to Exeter in the evening sunlight of 26 May 1986. *Philip J. Mason*

Right:
In Manchester orange and brown livery, two Class 142 two-car railbuses, Nos 142003 (leading) and 142001 are seen passing Bolton East signalbox on the 10.48am Manchester Victoria-Blackpool-North staff excursion train on 14 September 1985. *David A. Ingham*

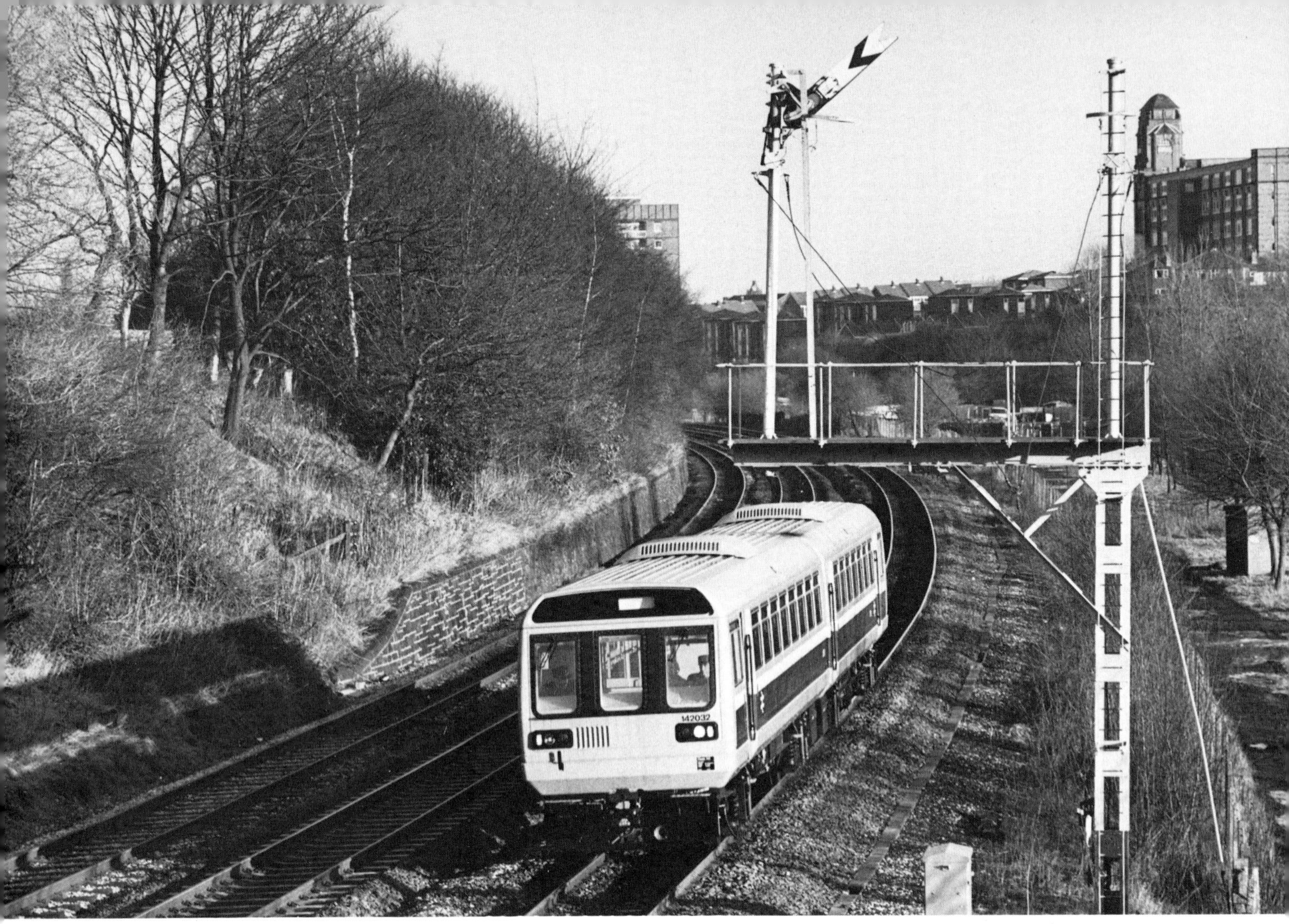
142032

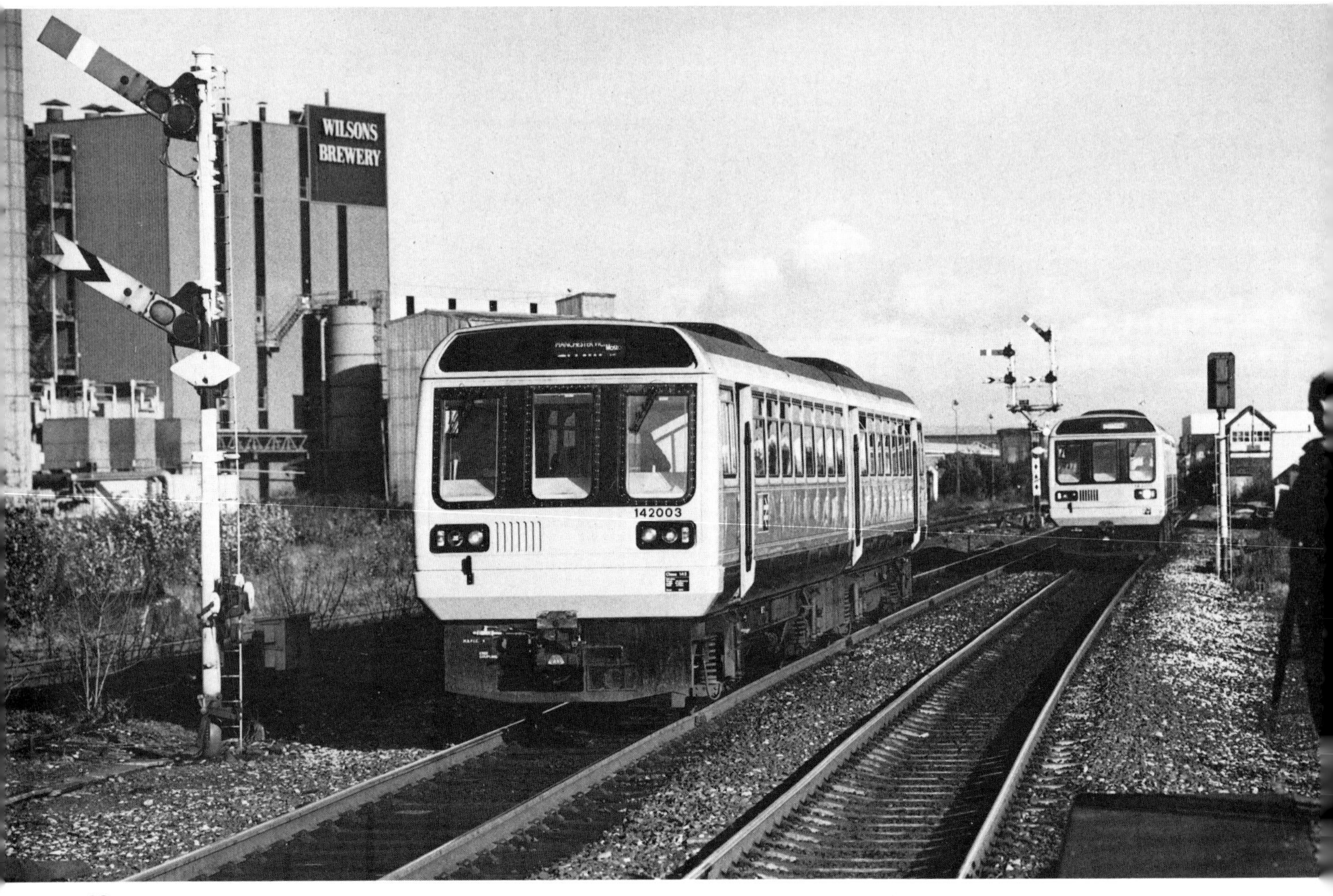
WILSONS
BREWERY
142003

Above left:

Viewed from certain angles — such as this — it is difficult not to think of road vehicles rather than trains. In Provincial Services two-tone blue livery, Class 142 No 142032 passes Lostock Junction, Bolton, on a driver-training run from Newton Heath to Blackpool on 25 January 1986. *David A. Ingham*

Left:

Two Pacers at Miles Platting station, Manchester, on 9 November 1985, both working on Manchester Victoria commuter services. No 142003 is on the left and 142001 is approaching on the right. *David A. Ingham*

Above:

Since the early 'New Generation' designs lack conventional guard's van luggage compartments, it is necessary for items such as bicycles to be carried in the doorway vestibules, where space is distinctly limited. The push button equipment for opening the doors can be seen here on DMS(L) No 55594 of unit 142003. *Ian Allan Library*

Right:

Close-up of the front end of Pacer railbus No 142011 in the Derby Litchurch Lane test house on 30 September 1985. The headlamp housings are open for inspection and some minor electrical work remains unfinished. *Colin J. Marsden*

11 W. Alexander/A. Barclay. Local & Secondary Services 2-Car. Class 143

Introduced: 1985
Purpose: Local & Secondary Services
No of Cars per Unit: 2
TOPS Class: 143
Engines: Leyland TL11 (2)
Horsepower: 410
Transmission: Mechanical
Body: DMS 15.11×2.73m, DMS (L) 15.37+2.73m
Unit Nos: 143001-143025
Brake Type: Electro-pneumatic
Max Unit Speed: 75mph
Coupling restrictions: With units of same class; also Classes 142, 144, 150/1, 150/2
Original Running Nos/Vehicle Type/Weight
55642-55666, DMS, 24 tonnes,
55667-55691, DMS(L), 25 tonnes.

The next 'new generation' DMU fleet designs to appear in BR Service, were the privately-built 'Pacers' known as Class 143, and constructed jointly by Walter Alexander of Falkirk (coach-builders) and the railway engineering firm of Andrew Barclay & Sons of Kilmarnock. This Scottish consortium had an original order for 25 two-car sets, but in the autumn of 1985 an additional order for 23 more sets was placed to follow on (these, Class 144 sets however, have BREL underframes and running gear, which means that Barclay have no further orders on hand). The first unit was ready by June 1985, but was immediately 'blacked' by the National Union of Railwaymen (NUR) until a High Court ruling sought by BR, forced the NUR to lift the 'blacking' of that year.

Once the NUR objection had been over-ruled the Class 143 railbuses started to arrive from the Andrew Barclay factory to Heaton depot, Tyneside, at the rate of one unit per week. After driver training, the Class 143s commenced work on the Newcastle-Sunderland and Middlesbrough-Newcastle services; to be followed by services from Newcastle to Hexham and Carlisle, Alnmouth and Durham. Initially, some test runs were made between Derby and Cricklewood, whilst the Derby Railway Technical Centre evaluated the new design.

The first units were finished in the new Provincial Services two-tone blue livery, but six of the first batch of units are painted in Tyne & Wear yellow and white; following a deal in which Tyne & Wear County Council paid for them. Cost of each two-car set is put at around £300,000. They can run in multiple with Classes 142, 144, 150/1 and 150/2. Beauty may well lie in the eye of the beholder, but in the present writer's opinion, these aluminium, wide-bodied railbuses are extremely attractive, and the front end design in particular is both clean and neat. They make a worthy addition to the 'new generation DMU fleet!

Below:
General arrangement of Class 143 Alexander/ Barclay Pacer railbus.

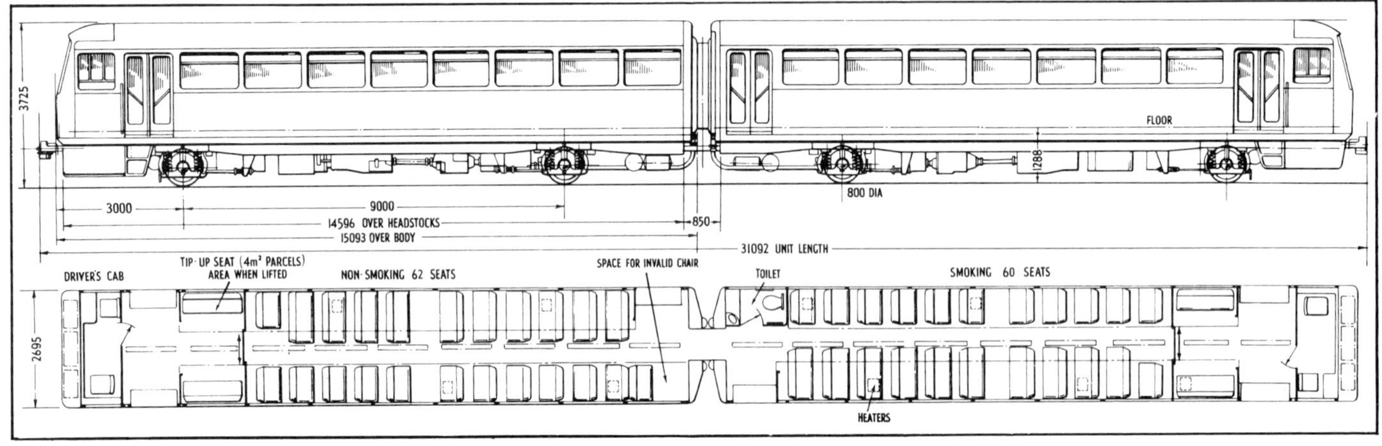

Left:
Unit No 143008, very much on home territory, is seen awaiting departure from Newcastle Central station with the 13.55 Newcastle-Sunderland on 25 February 1986. *C. J. Tuffs*

Above right:
Six Class 143 sets were paid for by Tyne & Wear Passenger Transport Executive and painted in the PTE's livery of yellow and white. The first of these six, No 143020, passes Monkwearmouth Station Museum with a Heworth-Sunderland special working conveying county councillors on 20 February 1986. *Ian S. Carr*

Right:
Three of the six Class 143 units in Tyne & Wear PTE livery are seen at Glaisdale on Sunday 27 July 1986. No 143020 brings up the rear of the 16.15 Middlesbrough-Whitby (led by No 143010, hidden from view), whilst Nos 143024 and 143023 form the 16.48 Whitby-Darlington. *Ian S. Carr*

Whitby
143020
143024

Above:
The Edinburgh-Bathgate line was reopened to passengers on 24 March 1986, with the service operated in part by several Class 143 units borrowed from Newcastle, a precursor of the intended future introduction of similar units in Scotland. Nos 143019 and 143016 arrive at Bathgate with the 13.18 from Edinburgh Waverley on the day following reopening, 25 March 1986. *T. H. Noble*

Below:
The first passenger train to use the new station under construction at Bishop Auckland was the 08.10 from Saltburn on Sunday 6 July 1986, formed of units Nos 143017 and 143007. *Ian S. Carr*

12 York Works BREL. Provincial Sector 2-Car. Class 150/1

Introduced: Provincial Services; Commuter and Cross-country.
No of Cars per Unit: 2
TOPS Class: 150/1
Engines: Cummins NT 855R5 of 285hp
Horsepower: 570
Transmission: Mechanical
Body: 19.84×2.82m
Unit Nos: 150101-150150
Brake Type: Electro-pneumatic
Max Unit Speed: 75mph
Coupling restrictions: Within units of same class, also Classes 142, 143, 144, 150/2.
Original running Nos/Vehicle type/Weight:
52101-52150, DMS(L) 38.45 tonnes.
57101-57150 DMS 38.45 tonnes.

The first production build of 'Sprinters' differs in one respect in that a two-car formation is used in place of the original three car layout. Otherwise, except for a modified livery, the original design is closely followed. Sets are gangwayed only at the inner end thus restricting passenger/guard movement whilst the train is in motion. Public address and driver-guard communication systems are, however, fitted, so that *audio* contact is possible throughout the journey when sets are working in multiple. It is not a perfect arrangement, in particular in the event of accident or emergency, and it is good news that a return to gangways throughout for future builds is now planned. However, one hopes that some consideration will be given to the appearance of these later 'Sprinters', because the gangway has certainly been a blemish on the face of recent BR EMU designs (317, 455, etc), whereas the non-gangwayed 'Sprinter' Class 150 has a reasonable appearance. Other criticisms are that valuable passenger accommodation is sometimes locked up (for security reasons) to carry a few parcels and that passengers with bicyles are not well catered for.

All of that said, the 'Sprinters' are nonetheless proving to be a huge success. On 20 January 1986, 37 of the new trains replaced almost all the old DMUs in the East Midlands — three months earlier than originally planned. Initially there was to have been no phasing-in period. All 50 of the first batch of 'Sprinters', costing £25 million, were to have entered full service at once, throughout the Midlands and North and mid-Wales in May 1986. Due to smart work by BREL York, enough of the Class 150/1 units were ready to enable the old, and virtually worn-out first generation DMUs to be shunted-into the sidings for the last time on 19 January 1986. The next morning 37 'Sprinter' sets based at Derby Etches Park depot took over all the services on the Lincoln-Nottingham-Birmingham/Crewe, Leicester-Birmingham and Derby-Matlock routes. Some of the class also worked to Grantham and Peterborough.

Since then, with more new units available the activities of the 'Sprinters' have been further extended, and in March 1986 an official launch of their use on the Cambrian lines in mid-Wales took place.

Below:
Members of the first production batch of BREL Sprinters (Class 150/1) differ from the Class 150 prototypes by the fact that they are two-car units. Externally, a finalised version of the Provincial Services two-tone blue gives a very smart look to their bodywork. Brand new unit No 150107 stands at Derby on 29 October 1985. *Alec Swain*

Above:
Without doubt the new 'Sprinters' have brightened up the prospects for provincial services, and given the public fresh opinions of diesel railcars in particular! Here the first of the many production sets is seen at York station, during trials on 26 September 1985. *Peter Harris*

Right:
Class 150/1 'Sprinter' No 150118 waits at Hinckley station in the early morning of the first day of Sprinter operations — 20 January 1986 — in the East Midlands area. The train is the 06.08 Lincoln Central-Birmingham New Street service. *Paul A. Biggs*

Below right:
Two days later, 22 January 1986, a pair of Class 150/1 units are seen approaching Burton-on-Trent station on the 14.40 Nottingham-Birmingham New Street working. Unit No 150135 leads, with No 150118 at the rear. *C. J. Tuffs*

Left:
From April 1986 the production build of Class 150/1 'Sprinters' also took over regular passenger duties on the Cambrian lines west of Shrewsbury. On 18 April No 150109 is seen near Shrewsbury with the 11.40 Crewe-Pwhelli. *C. J. Tuffs*

Below:
Three Class 150/1 units forming a special train from Shrewsbury to Barmouth on 13 April 1986 skirt the coast near Aberdovey. *G. F. Bannister*

13 W. Alexander/BREL Derby. Local & Secondary Services 2-Car. Class 144

Introduced: 1986
Purpose: Local & Secondary Services
No of Cars per Unit: 2
TOPS Class: 144
Engines: Leyland TL11 (2)
Horsepower: 410
Transmission: Mechanical
Body: DMS 15.11×2.73m, DMS(L) 15.37×2.73m
Unit Nos: 144001-144023
Brake type: Electro-pneumatic
Maximum speed: 75mph
Coupling restrictions: With units of same class; also Classes 142, 143, 150/1, 150/2
Running Nos/Vehicle Type/Weight: 55801-55823, DMS, 55824-55846, DMS(L)

The 23 members of Class 144 are very similar in design and construction to Class 143. As with Class 143 the bodies were built by Walter Alexander, but the chassis for the Class 144 units came from BREL at Derby. The first unit was delivered in September 1986, running trials in the Derby area and on the Midland main line. All members of the class were allocated to Neville Hill depot at Leeds, for use in West Yorkshire.

Below:
No 144001, first member of the class, is seen as new at Derby Works. Certain items such as footsteps remain to be fitted. The resemblance to Class 143 is apparent. *British Rail*

Bottom:
On 4 September 1986 the brand new No 144001 was photographed near Spondon while on test, returning to Derby from Cricklewood. *C. J. Tuffs*

14 British Leyland/BREL Derby. Local & Secondary Services 2-Car. Class 142/1.

Introduced: 1986
Purpose: Local and secondary services
No of Cars per Unit: 2
TOPS Class: 142/1
Engines: Leyland TL11 (2)
Horsepower: 410
Transmission: Mechanical SCG
Body: 15.66×2.8m
Unit Nos: 142101-142146
Brake type: Electro-pneumatic
Maximum speed: 75mph
Coupling restrictions: With units of same class
Running Nos/Vehicle Type/Weight: 55701-55746 DMS, 55747-55792 DMS(L)

Following the first 50 members of Class 142, a further batch of 46 units known as Class 142/1 was ordered. Again they came from the Associated Rail Technologies team of Leyland and BREL Derby. Although it had been expected that this second batch would be numbered 142101-142146, in fact they carried numbers continuing the sequence from the initial 50 units. The first Class 142/1 representative, No 142051, appeared in September 1986. The first 20 sets were due to be allocated to Newton Heath depot at Manchester for services in Lancashire, with the remaining 26 going to Neville Hill depot, Leeds.

Below:
First of the Class 142/1 series, No 142051 is seen at Liverpool Lime Street station on the occasion of the inauguration of the Preston-Liverpool 'Pacer' service on 25 September 1986. The unit is almost identical in appearance with the first 50 Class 142 units.
R. Cragg

15 York Works BREL. Provincial Sector 2-Car. Class 150/2

Introduced: 1986
Purpose: Provincial Services, Commuter and Cross-country
No of Cars per Unit: 2
TOPS Class: 150/2
Engines: Cummins NT 855R5 (2)
Horsepower: 570
Transmission: Mechanical
Body: 19.84×2.82m
Unit Nos: 150201-150285
Brake type: Electro-pneumatic
Maximum speed: 75mph
Coupling restrictions: With units of same class; also Classes 142, 143, 144, 150/1
Running Nos/Vehicle Type/Weight: 52201-52285, DMS(L), 57201-57285, DMS

In most respects very similar to the members of Class 150/1, Class 150/2 units differ fundamentally in having through gangways fitted between units as well as within sets. This difference is readily apparent due to the revised cab design incorporating corridor connections. The first example, No 150201, emerged from BREL York Works in late September 1986, going first to Derby for tests. Mechanically Class 150/2 is fully compatible with the preceding units but the end gangways give much greater operational flexibility, particularly with the unit formation for production 'Sprinters' having been reduced to two cars from the three of the prototypes.

Above:
The first member of Class 150/2, No 150201, emerged from BREL York in September 1986 and was sent to Derby where it was displayed with other new items of rolling stock. After this it returned to York for final work to be carried out prior to entering service. The major visible alteration from the previous 'Sprinter' units was the fitting of end gangway connections, with a front end design almost identical with that of the latest suburban EMU designs. The unit was turned out carrying a reversed form of Provincial Sector blue and grey livery, with the light blue band at waist level and dark blue around the carriage windows. The 'Sprinter' motif clearly visible on the vehicle bodyside was an innovation not previously used. Although No 150201 surprisingly appeared without standard yellow cab ends, it was expected that these would be applied before the unit entered service. *British Rail*

16 York Works BREL. General Purpose Prototype 3-Car. Class 154.

Introduced: 1986
Purpose: General duties, ranging from commuter services to cross-country and secondary main line services
No of Cars per Unit: 2/3
TOPS Class: 154
Engines: Cummins (2)
Horsepower: 700/1,050
Transmission: Mechanical SCG
Body: 19.93×2.73m
Unit No: 154001
Brake type: Electro-pneumatic
Maximum speed: 90mph
Coupling restrictions: With units of Classes 150/0, 151

Running Nos/Vehicle Type/Weight: 55201 DMS, 35.4 tonnes, 55301 DMS, 34.7 tonnes 55401 MBD, 35 tonnes

Notes: Rebuilt from Class 150/0 No 150002 as the prototype of 'Super Sprinter' with air-conditioning and a 90mph capability.

In 1986 work started at Derby RTC to convert No 150002, one of the two prototype 'Sprinters', into a test-bed for equipment to be used on future 'Super Sprinters'. No 154001 would run initially as a two-car train, although it was expected that the third car would be available from May 1987.

The conversion involved fitting the two driving vehicles, Nos 55201 and 55301 with standard 'Sprinter' Cummins engines, uprated to 350hp by the addition of an intercooler. This would raise the maximum speed from 75mph to 90mph and also power air conditioning equipment — the first 'Sprinter' so fitted. The transmission used on 55201 was to be an uprated Voith type similar to the production 'Sprinters' whilst 55301 would have a twin disk torque convertor as fitted to the two Class 151 prototypes. The SCG final drive units were to be retained, but regeared for 90mph operation.

The increased maximum speed required an additional damper to be fitted to the bogies.

Air conditioning equipment would consist of a compressor and condenser mounted on the underframe, with an evaporator unit contained in the roof. All hopper window ventilators would be sealed off, except for two per vehicle retained for emergency use.

17 Leyland. Provincial Sector 2-Car. Class 155.

Introduced: 1987
Purpose: Long-distance provincial services
No of Cars per Unit: 2
TOPS Class: 155
Engines: Cummins NT 855R5 of 285hp
Horsepower: 570
Transmission: Mechanical
Body: 23m length
Unit Nos: 155301-155335
Brake type: Electro-pneumatic
Maximum speed:
Coupling restrictions: With units of same class
Running Nos/Vehicle Type/Weight: 52301-52335 DMS(L), 57301-57335 DMS

Following the initial orders for production 'Sprinters' of the 150 family, based on the two successful prototypes Nos 150001/2, it was decided that a requirement existed for longer bodied units for Provincial Sector services. As a result orders were placed for series construction of two new Sprinter designs with 23m length vehicles.

The first of these was placed with Leyland for 35 two-car Class 155 units, to be introduced in 1987. It was anticipated that these would feature 2+2 seating, being intended for longer distance cross-country services.

18 Metropolitan-Cammell. Provincial Sector 2-Car. Class 156.

Introduced: 1987
Purpose: Long-distance provincial services
No of Cars per Unit: 2
TOPS Class: 156
Engines: Cummins NT 855R5 of 285hp
Horsepower: 570
Transmission: Mechanical
Body: 23m length
Unit Nos: 156401-156514
Brake type: Electro-pneumatic
Maximum speed:
Coupling restrictions: With units of same class

Running Nos/Vehicle Type/Weight: 52401-52514 DMS(L), 57401-57514 DMS

In addition to the Class 155 Leyland units, no fewer than 114 two-car 23m 'Sprinters' were ordered from Metro-Cammell, these being Class 156. This substantial order was perhaps some consolation for the stylish Class 151 design not having been ordered for series production. The Class 156 Metro-Cammell units were to the same basic specification as the Leyland 23m unit order, with delivery likewise due to commence during 1987.

Future Construction

Although the initial deliveries of 'Second Generation' DMUs have had a dramatic effect on the face of local and provincial services, much more is to come; so that between 1986 and 1990 more than £300 million is planned to be invested by BR to replace the first generation DMU fleet. The allocation of authorised 1986/87 vehicle builds is shown in the accompanying table.

	Quantity:	*Depot:*	*Intended delivery:*
Class: 150/2	62	Cardiff	September 86
	60	Newton Heath	November 86
	48	Neville Hill	March 87
Class: 155	70	Cardiff	April 87
Class: 156	30	Inverness	Not yet defined
	64	ScR (South)	
	60	Newton Heath	
	40	Norwich	
	34	Neville Hill	

Details of these orders, together with the Class 154 prototype 90mph 'Sprinter' (converted from unit No 150002) appear on pages 78 and 79. Each of the new classes represents a refinement of the basic Class 150 family. Class 150/2 incorporates inter-unit gangways, whilst Classes 155 and 156 are the first to be built to 23m body length, and also feature a revised internal layout. The omission of Classes 152 and 153 allows for any subsequent orders of 20m vehicle units to a new design.

APPENDIX
Southern Region DEMU Renumbering

From mid-1986 all Southern Region DEMUs in service were renumbered to carry a six-figure TOPS number. The first three figures of this consist of the class designation, with the remaining three giving the individual unit identity. Thus No 1401, the first member of Class 204, became No 204001.

Members of a sub-class include this information as the fourth figure of the new number. For example, the first member of Class 205/0, originally numbered 1101, became No 205001; whilst the only member of Class 205/1; formerly No 1111, became No 205101.

Class	*Original Numbers*	*New Numbers*
202	1013	202001
203	1011	203001
204	1401-1404	204001-204004
205/0	1101-1110	205001-205010
	1112	205012
	1114-1133	20514-205033
205/1	1111	205101
206/1	1113	206101
207	1301-1319	207001-207019

Below:
Class 207 unit No 207005 (formerly No 1307) clearly shows the newly-applied TOPS unit number on 12 July 1986, leaving Hurst Green with the East Grinstead portion of the 12.36 from Victoria. *Alex Dasi-Sutton*